Madonna

the
Complete
Guide *to her*
Music

OMNIBUS PRESS
London/New York
Paris/Sydney/Copenhagen
Berlin/Madrid/Tokyo

Rikky Rooksby

Cover and book designed by Chloë Alexander
Picture research by Sarah Bacon

ISBN: 0.7119.9883.3
Order No: OP49500

Exclusive Distributors
Book Sales Limited
8/9 Frith Street,
London W1D 3JB, UK.

Music Sales Corporation
257 Park Avenue South,
New York, NY 10010, USA.

Music Sales Pty Limited,
120 Rothschild Avenue, Rosebery,
NSW 2018, Australia.

To the Music Trade only:
Music Sales Limited,
8/9, Frith Street,
London W1D 3JB, UK.

Photo credits:
Every effort has been made to trace the copyright holders of
the photographs in this book but one or two were
unreachable. We would be grateful if the photographers
concerned would contact us.

Printed by: Cox & Wyman Ltd, Reading, Berks.

A catalogue record for this book is available from the British
Library.

Visit Omnibus Press at http://www.musicsales.co.uk

Contents

INTRODUCTION

*'When I was tiny my grandmother used to beg me not to go with boys,
to love Jesus and be a good girl. I grew up with two images of women:
the Virgin and the whore.'* (Madonna)

*'I sometimes think I was born to live up to my name. How could I be
anything else but what I am having been named Madonna? I would
either have ended up as a nun or this.'* (Vanity Fair, 1991)

'In many respects she's the perfect pop artist.' (George Michael)

MADONNA IS THE MOST SUCCESSFUL FEMALE SINGER IN THE HISTORY OF
popular music. In the Eighties only U2, Prince, Michael Jackson and
Springsteen could rival her success. From 1984 onwards she dominated pop
music, appearing to transcend and cross all kinds of boundaries of language
and culture. Her record sales are well over the 100 million mark and still rising. Twenty years after her first hit single, a new Madonna record still enters
high on the charts across the world. Of course, commercial pulling-power
and record sales do not necessarily offer any indication of the lasting affection people can feel for a performer and his or her music. Many million-selling albums soon clutter up the bargain bins because the music has not
proved to have a lasting hold on people's hearts. Whether people hold her in
as much affection as they do other musical greats has yet to be seen. But in
2004 it seems they do.

The magnitude of Madonna's success is the product of a range of
factors, great and small, entered into a unique equation. Like David Bowie in
the Seventies, she is a master of the art of re-inventing herself by changing
her image. She has always understood the importance of image, how it
communicates in the world of pop, and has ransacked the fashions of the
twentieth century to present a kaleidoscope of personae. She understands
that in the pop game the highest levels of success are sustained only by
staying one step ahead of competitors and holding the attention of a public
that has plenty of other distractions. Her hair changes colour frequently, her
clothes have gone from junkshop mix-and-match to Fifties glamour and
just about everything in between. She has had no reservations about
marketing herself as a sex symbol in order to attract male attention.

Perhaps more importantly, something about her chimed with the
female audience who attended her concerts in droves, wore similar clothes
to the Material Girl, and now in their thirties are still having vividly symbolic
dreams about her, as catalogued in Kay Turner's book *I Dream of Madonna*.

A generation of young women identified with her rebellious attitude, and with the bold statement that women could be mistress of their destinies and sexy at the same time. Her records have not only moved the feet of these women but stirred their hearts and their ambitions. Madonna's rise to fame is a rags-to-riches story grafted onto a feminist fairy-tale about a young woman who fights her way to the top of a man's world... except that contrary to the militant feminism of the late Sixties and Seventies, she's intent on looking great when she gets there.

This aspect of Madonna can be summed up in the phrase, 'blond ambition'. Many believe her success is mostly down to calculation and the ability to sacrifice others at the right moment for the sake of her career - which is pretty much what men have been doing in business for years. It's a notorious double standard. If a man is ambitious and ruthless, he's a powerful, decisive go-getter; if a woman exhibits the same qualities, she's a bitch. For this reason, Bette Midler's remark at Live Aid about Madonna being a woman who pulled herself up by her own bra-straps (and occasionally let them down), though witty, was in poor taste. At that time various pornographic magazines were publishing nude photographs of Madonna without her consent. Madonna's performance before a global audience that day was feisty. She took on the challenge of the moment and danced with exuberant defiance in front of an audience that was predominantly there to see the old warhorses of rock lumber through their familiar gestures. It was the classic confrontation between the audience that was still hanging to the last shreds of the notion of rock as counter-culture and a performer with a new line in taking on the status quo. To them, she was an upstart, a hype, a chart bubble that would soon burst and evaporate into obscurity. They were wrong. Madonna was going to become as much a part of the history of popular music as anyone else on the bill that day on either side of the Atlantic. She emerged from the event unbowed and unbeaten.

Whatever cynics say, image and hype alone do not generate such success. On the sleeve of one of her more recent albums, *Something To Remember* (1995), Madonna complains that her music hardly ever gets any attention. This is undeniably true. Of course she has largely created this state of affairs herself: she has courted publicity as a star first and foremost, rather than a singer or writer, through her image, her interviews, her films, her videos, and her every paparazzi-festooned move. She has been dubbed 'Our Lady of Perpetual Promotion' as well as the 'Pop poet of lower middle-class America', and the former role has tended to eclipse the latter. What Madonna has relentlessly promoted is her own myth, not her music. She says she believes 'Art should be controversial... It should make people think about what they do and don't believe in. It's good to get people to question their beliefs, their values. So much music and entertainment today just puts people in a trance', a statement which shows her belief in the importance of the music. It seems that at every step of her career some extra-musical issue arises which, although guaranteed to shift units, diverts attention from what goes in the words of the song into the groove.

First, there was her initial image: the bare navel, the just-out-of-bed hair, dripping with cheap jewellery and crucifixes, the incarnation of the Eighties material girl. This gave way to the coy bump'n'grind of songs such as 'Like A Virgin', sung in a manner making clear she was anything but. Then there was the controversy over the lyrics of 'Papa Don't Preach' - was it pro-abortion or pro-life or pro-sales? - her tempestuous romance, marriage, and divorce with actor Sean Penn, closely followed by the hoo-ha over videos such as 'Like A Prayer' and 'Justify My Love', the latter promptly notching up something like 440,000 sales in a few months as a single video in its own right. There was her book *Sex*, certainly the sleaziest move of her career, and her film *Truth Or Dare/In Bed With Madonna*, with its revelations of life on the road. There has been critical acclaim for her portrayal of Eva Peron in *Evita*, motherhood, marriage, *Swept Away*, electronica, and her children's story *The English Rose*. Finally, there is the confusing fact that she makes films, inviting audiences to wonder with each successive role, "Is she really like that?" At times it has seemed like she's an actress who happens to make the occasional record rather than the other way round.

So Madonna's music is rarely discussed. Looking at the books about her, it is staggering how little comment is passed on the music, let alone on how it was conceived and made. Never before in the field of popular music has a performer been so successful and their music had so little analysis. To some, the very notion of trying to discuss Madonna's music - rather than the colour of her hair, the contents of her wardrobe or who she was seen with last night - would seem to be a contradictory notion. What music? Madonna, so they say, equals the triumph of style over content. She makes dance-pop with airhead lyrics repeated over an endlessly repeating beat. End of story. But there have been some dissenting voices. In his book *The Heart of Rock and Soul - The Thousand Greatest Singles Ever Made* - rock critic Dave Marsh included half a dozen of Madonna's singles, and made it very clear that he thought she was neglected as a musical talent. When her 1989 album *Like A Prayer* was released, *Rolling Stone* went as far as to call it the 'closest pop ever gets to art'.

So what gives? Is Madonna the ultimate in disposable pop or is there more to her music than meets the eye? And when we talk about Madonna's music - whose music are we talking about? Madonna's records depend upon the talent and input of a range of people, more so than with most artists. The majority of her songs are collaborations with associates like Patrick Leonard, Steve Bray, William Orbit and Mirwais Ahmadzai, amongst others. It has not always been easy to identify exactly what Madonna's contribution to her records has been. It appears that she writes the words and the melody and sometimes the chord sequences. But a significant proportion of the music has come from other people.

Contrary to early popular prejudice, a careful listen to her records certainly demonstrates musical growth and progression. From 'Holiday' to 'This Used To Be My Playground', 'Erotica' or 'What It Feels Like For A Girl' is a huge step for anyone. She started as a dance artist, her music little more than a slice of rhythm to get people to bounce on the dancefloors of a million clubs. From there it became party music. She embraced pop music more, moved away from dance, drew heavily on her Sixties influences, took care to deal with personal issues in her lyrics and came up with the *Like A Prayer* album. Her film career led to her most sophisticated move to date in 1990 when she tried her hand at various Twenties/Thirties pastiche ballads and light jazz tunes for the film *Dick Tracy*.

In the Nineties she stayed contemporary by using elements of the electronic dance/house/hip-hop/rap scene, making her music sound tougher and up-to-date. The *Something To Remember* collection of some of her slower ballad material with a few new songs marked time. Early in her career critics like Dennis Hunt of the *LA Times* compared her to Little Bo Peep, 'with her bleating vibrato, it sometimes makes her sound like a sheep in pain'. Certainly the singer on tracks like 'Rain' or 'You'll See' had come a long way from the shrill, high-pitched voice of her early hits. It suggested that creatively at least she was biding her time, perhaps unsure of where to go next. Then in 1998 *Ray Of Light* revitalized her career, to be followed by *Music* and *American Life*. This trio of albums have given her another brace of hit singles to add to an already staggering list.

What follows in this guide will enable you to view her music in a new light. She has always essentially been a singles artist which is reflected in her astonishing run of hits. Her output has also been affected by the phenomena of re-mixes - so that rather than provide new material there has been a tendency for her to recycle her work rather than create new material. This is evident on her singles, especially the 12" formats, but also on an album like *You Can Dance* and even on *Something To Remember*. Whatever the importance of re-mixes in dance music, it certainly chimes very well with the economics of record company finances and profit boosting. It is much more costly to record a new song than re-mix one you already have in the can. But Madonna is really a pop singer, and some of her work has been damaged by over-long song times.

In the six years since the first edition of this book there has been plenty of new music from Madonna, as witnessed by three studio albums, a second volume of greatest hits, several songs for films (including a Bond song), and her fifth tour. This revised edition reviews these releases, as well marking the extended lease of life given to past releases courtesy of new formats such as DVD. In 2001 her first four albums were remastered with the addition of a couple of different mixes. *The Immaculate Conception* is available as an SACD. 'Music' and 'What It Feels Like For A Girl' exist in DVD single format. The *American Life* album was 'enhanced'. More Madonna will appear as DVD-audio and 5.1 sound. It looks like the Material Girl's music will be with us for a long time to come.

In the preparation of this guide magazines like *Record Collector* and *Q* have been a useful source of information. In addition, the biographies of Madonna by Robert Matthew-Walker (1989), Mark Bego (1991), and Christopher Andersen (1991), Andrew Morton (2001), plus Fred Bronson's *Billboard Book of U.S. Hits, Madonna: In Her Own Words*, and *The Madonna Scrapbook* by Lee Randall (1992) have been helpful. I would also like to thank the press-office at WEA, London for allowing me to consult their extensive files of material on Madonna.

Rikky Rooksby, October 2003

THE ALBUMS
Madonna / The First Album

Original UK issue: Sire 9238671, released September 1983;

CD Sire 923867-2.

Retitled with a new cover as Sire WX 22, September 1985

MADONNA'S JOURNEY TO MAKING HER FIRST RECORD WAS AS RAGS-TO-RICHES as anyone's. Born Madonna Ciccione, she was the third of six children with Italian-American parents. Her father worked at the Chrysler car factory near Detroit. Her sensibility was shaped by Roman Catholicism and the need to both acknowledge and rebel against it has run through much of her music. The trauma of her mother dying when Madonna was only six is also a major influence in her life and work . She grew up absorbing a variety of popular music and looking to Hollywood screen goddesses like Monroe for inspiration. She did ballet and by the end of her teens had the choice of either a scholarship in dance at Michigan University or dance tuition at a studio in New York. She went to New York for a few months, met musician Dan Gilroy and got involved in practical music-making. She spent some time playing drums. Gradually, she learned how to survive in a vibrant but sometimes threatening environment. She did various dead-end jobs to make a few dollars, including some nude modelling. These photographs would return to haunt her in years to come.

The first real break came not long after her Detroit boyfriend Steve Bray came over to New York to be the drummer in the band. They abandoned hard rock, got signed by a music management company, decided to pursue a more funked-up groove, and then left the said company. They had rough tapes of three songs: 'Everybody', 'Ain't No Big Deal' and 'Burning Up'. The next task was to find a way to test these songs on the public. Madonna pressed a tape of these tracks into the hands of Mark Kamins, a DJ at the Dancetaria Club, one of the clubs where she used to go dancing. He played 'Everybody' and it got a great reaction from the crowd. Kamins decided he should try to get her a record deal on the understanding that he would get to produce it.

This led to an approach in 1982 to Sire Records. Michael Rosenblatt was part of the A&R department at Sire and commented, "Madonna is great. She will do anything to be a star, and that's exactly what I look for in an artist: total co-operation... With Madonna, I knew I had someone hot and co-operative, so I planned to build her career with singles, rather than just put an album out right away and run the risk of disaster."

Seymour Stein, President of Sire, was also impressed, and signed her for two 12" singles. Mark Kamins produced a 12" of 'Everybody' that lasted 5:56 on one side with a 9:23 dub version on the flip. It was released in April 1982 and became a huge dance hit. This led to talk of doing an album. Madonna opted not to work with either Kamins or Bray but went instead for Reggie Lucas, a Warner Brothers producer. Lucas pushed her in more of a pop direction, cutting 'Burning Up' / 'Physical Attraction' which was released in March 1983 and made number 3 in the dance charts. Although it wasn't a pop hit, the video for the single caused a minor stir on MTV.

From the start of her career, Madonna understood the power of video, and admits that, "If I didn't have a video, I don't think all the kids in the Midwest would know about me. It takes the place of touring. Everybody sees them everywhere. That really has a lot to do with the success of my album."

When Madonna went into the studio to make her first album she did not have much material to play with. What was available was 'Lucky Star', a new version of 'Ain't No Big Deal', 'Think Of Me' and 'I Know It'. George Lucas brought two songs to the project, 'Physical Attraction' and 'Borderline'. As he recorded the tracks he decorated them, moving them away from the sparse form of the original demo versions. This change was not to Madonna's liking, so 'Jellybean' Benitez was called in to re-mix the tracks. Benitez was a DJ at the Funhouse disco and was making a name for himself as a producer. He said of Madonna, "I thought she had a lot of style, and she crossed over a lot of boundaries because everyone in the rock clubs played her – the black clubs, the gay, the straight – and very few records have that appeal". He put extra guitars and some new vocal parts on 'Burning Up' and 'Lucky Star'. Critically for Madonna's success, Steve Bray had sold his song 'Ain't No Big Deal' to an act on another label, rendering it unavailable for Madonna's project. The team therefore needed to find a new potential hit, and discovered the necessary gem in the form of a Hudson/ Stevens song which had been turned down by Mary Wilson, formerly of The Supremes. The track was cut in a week, with Jellybean spending four frantic days after the vocal was laid down trying to enhance the commercial appeal of the song. The intention had been that 'Lucky Star' would be the, lead release but when 'Holiday' became the US number 1 dance record, it naturally became the single. Legend has it that the original sleeve didn't carry a picture of Madonna because the record company didn't want people to find out too soon that she wasn't black.

The album clearly shows the haste with which it was made. If you have the singles or *The Immaculate Collection* then you can live without it.

The overall sound of the record is dissonant, upbeat synthetic disco, utilising some of the new technology of the time like the Linn drum machine, Moog bass, the OB-X synthesiser, equipment which has since dated, and consequently now sounds rather harsh. In this respect, Madonna's early recordings have suffered in the same way as many of the disco / new romantic bands who were her contemporaries.

The first album is really musical candyfloss – okay in the right spot at the right time. Madonna has said of her debut that "the songs were pretty weak and I went to England during the recordings so I wasn't around... I wasn't in control", and that "I didn't realise how crucial it was for me to break out of the disco mould before I'd nearly finished the [first] album. I wish I could have got a little more variety there."

The tracks 'Holiday', 'Everybody' and 'Physical Attraction' were later re-mixed for the album, *You Can Dance* (1987).

LUCKY STAR
(Madonna)

A SPARKLE OF synth notes starts off this medium-paced dance track. Most of the ingredients of Madonna's early sound are here: the cutesy voice which drew comparisons with Cyndi Lauper; the heavy electronic drums with strong emphasis on the backbeat reinforced with handclaps (again electronic); the flickering soul guitar licks and the trademark bubbling bass synth. The lyrics were repetitive and inane, here revolving around the transparent ambiguity of the star /heavenly body image. The song never takes too long to return to the hook, though perhaps goes on about a minute too long - although this may not be the case if you're dancing to it. This song gave Madonna the first of her 15 US top five hits (a triumph which beats the shared record of The Beatles and Elvis Presley). The B-side of the twice released single is 'You'll Know It'.

BORDERLINE
(R. Lucas)

L IKE THE opening track, 'Borderline' has a pretty intro, this time provided by keyboards. Anthony Jackson, the renowned session bass player, apparently played on this track, but it is not easy to hear his contribution. Madonna is again singing in her higher register.

This is probably the most harmonically complex track on the album. It has quite a few chord inversions which look back to Seventies disco, to the sound of Philadelphia, and to mid-Seventies Elton John, musical techniques which were not to become part of her musical style. The chord sequence for the verse may also have you thinking of Bachman Turner Overdrive's 'You Ain't Seen

Nothing Yet'!

The short synth phrases that interlock throughout are typical of her style. The video for 'Borderline' was the first to get Madonna extensive exposure and caused her to be recognised in public for the first time in her life. This track was her third single, with 'Physical Attraction' on the flip, and was a top 10 hit in the US.

ly typewriter drive belts. The video became a minor hit on MTV, the station which started broadcasting 24 hour music in the early Eighties and was to play an important role in Madonna's career as a new stage on which to perform, a platform from which she could reach a vast audience. The song was used as background music for a scene in the film *Wild Life* (1984).

BURNING UP
(Madonna)

THIS WAS Madonna's second single, and reached number 3 in the US dance chart.

Noticeably weaker than the first two tracks, 'Burning Up' has a starker arrangement, carried mostly by the bass, single guitar, and drum machine. It sounds very much like the disco end of new romanticism, and could almost be Gary Numan. The loud tom-tom fills a la Phil Collins and guitar solo featured on this tack were not to become characteristics of Madonna's records.

The chorus is a repetition of the same three lines, whilst the bridge is a series of double entendres about what she is prepared to do for her lover, as she is not like the others and has no shame. All in all, the songs cold mechanical lack of groove is entirely at odds with the prolaimed passion and abandon of the lyric.

The colourful video for this single helped to cement Madonna's, featuring her wearing the famous rubber bracelets which were actual-

I KNOW IT
(Madonna)

SIDE 1 OF the vinyl and tape versions of Madonna's début album comes to an end with a song that has a gentler swing to it. Stabbing piano chords, a few swirling synth phrases, a sax flourish, carry the two-chord verse which then modulates to a different minor-based sequence on the chorus. The slightly offbeat chord changes in this tune cause Madonna no problem in the vocal department. Again, this is not a musical direction that she was going to follow. Her technique of harmonising with herself on the chorus of this song as though she were her own girl group backing was one which she would later develop.

HOLIDAY
(C. Hudson/L. Stevens)

OR SHOULD it be called Madonna Attacks!? For a few months in 1984 it seemed like you couldn't possibly escape this record. You could go hiking in Vancouver, chase kangaroos in the outback, go surfing in the Pacific or mingle with the crowds of Bombay, and it seemed you'd still hear Madonna's shrill cry of "it would be so nice!!" 'Holiday' was about as infectious as the plague. One listen and you couldn't get the damn hook out of your mind. The track starts with a chord sequence reminiscent of Cyndi Lauper's 'Time After Time' and most of it is based on a four-bar sequence which just keeps moving around. Madonna's success with this song stems from the fact that it expresses a universal sentiment. Let's face it, I need a holiday, you need a holiday, we all need a holiday! A Chic-style guitar flickers away in the background, the electronic handclaps never get sore, and synthesised strings add just the right touches of glamour to the melody. After a couple of minutes it becomes clear that the track has no structure. The song is in effect a prolonged chorus.

You're either on this six-minute carousel or you're getting nauseous watching it go round and round. You pays your money and takes your choice. The only thing that changes is the arrangement, like the piano break that comes toward the end. The song entered the *Billboard* Top 100 in the week of October 29, 1983 and had reached number 16 by February of the following year. 'Think Of Me' was on the B side. 'Holiday' was re-released in 1991 with 'True Blue' and charted again.

THINK OF ME
(Madonna)

A SINGLE high piano note starts this track before the drums . It's another tune that looks back to late Seventies disco. A short verse punctuated by a low synth bass figure very quickly leads into a chorus that gets in the regulation triple repeat of the song title. Madonna warns her erring lover that he'd better pay her some attention or she'll be out the door, a sentiment that a fair percentage of her female audience would certainly be able to identify with. Toward the end a bit of spurious interest is injected by messing about with the mix. The snare-drum is pulled out of the mix too, leaving the bass line and handclaps to keep things ticking over, while a sax takes a solo. We then return to the chorus. Life is short. You needn't hear this.

PHYSICAL ATTRACTION
(R. Lucas)

OR THIS. Another medium-paced track with synth bass right to the fore, a Chic guitar line, and a few synth brass flourishes, and Madonna singing in her shrillest voice about a suitor who she knows is probably no good for her but is attracted to anyway. Guess what? It's a...physical attraction. Yaay!

The verses are quite repetitive but the song does make it to a bridge with a few Collins-style drum fills panned across the stereo field. She even gets a talking section in, a forerunner of the technique she employs on tracks like 'Erotica': she wants him and it's nothing to be ashamed of. This is really a dance track more than a song as the length (6:35) indicates. It became the B-side of 'Burning Up', Madonna's second single.

EVERYBODY
(Madonna)

THIS WAS Madonna's first single. Her fifth composition closes her début album on something of a flat note. A heavily synthesised intro and a spoken introduction, with a loud intake of breath (!) leads to an invitation to get up and dance, repeated constantly. The sound is artificial, repetitive and uninspired. And it goes on and on and on... with Madonna's voice in gum-chewing mode and double-tracked for your added pleasure. Difficult to believe that when DJ Mark Kamins played an early version of this at the Dancetaria Club it got a very favourable response. What were they on? This was the song which was presented to Sire early in 1982. As Uncle Chuck once opined, you never can tell...

Like A Virgin

Original UK Issue: Sire 9251571, CD 925175-2

Released November 1984; Re-issued with additional track Sire WX 20,
CD 925181-2 August 1985

FOR THIS FOLLOW-UP ALBUM MADONNA CALLED ON THE SONGWRITING TALENTS of old friend Steve Bray. The aim was to make a stronger, more pop album than her debut which had been made in a rush. To sustain momentum, the material was going to have to be better quality and the record needed to be sweeter on this ears. To this end Nile Rodgers of the group Chic was brought in to produce. He was a hot ticket at the time, having done sterling work at the controls on David Bowie's *Let's Dance* and Paul Simon's *Hearts And Bones*. With him came some of the Power Station musicians, notably Bernard Edwards on bass and Tony Thompson on drums.

The inclusion of such experienced musicians did not mean that Madonna had abandoned the high-tech side of music-making. Equipment such as electronic drums by Linn and Simmons, the Synclavier II and Juno 60 synthesisers were employed and as the sleeve note added, the music was "fanatically recorded digitally from start to finish on Sony equipment". Sessions went on at the Power Station in New York. Madonna stated that she had "a lot more confidence in myself and I had a lot more to do with the way it came out soundwise". The sessions were completed in April 1984 but release of the album was held up, much to Madonna's frustration, by the continuing sales of her debut, which by now had achieved million-selling status in the US.

By the start of 1985 *Like A Virgin*, its title track, and the accompanying video were dominating the charts, and the video made her a fixture on MTV.

Like A Virgin is not that much of a musical departure from the first album, though the material is generally stronger. The album was re-issued with 'Into The Groove' added after that song had become a hit single following its use in the film *Desperately Seeking Susan* (1985), a suprise box office success in which Madonna plays a character not a million miles from herself. The inclusion of 'Into The Groove' definitely strengthened the record. Madonna candidly described *Like A Virgin* as "a much harder album, much more aggressive than the first record. The songs on that were pretty weak. On this one I've chosen all the songs and I want them all to be hits - no fillers. That's why I've done outside songs as well as six of my own... I wanted every song to be strong."

Whatever its musical merits or lack of them, there's no denying that

Like A Virgin has attained some significance as a cultural artefact of the Eighties. Whether Madonna wished this or not, the album captured the trashy, hedonistic materialism of the 'Me' Decade and made her its patron saint. Madonna is posed on the cover in a wedding costume which has been subtly altered. The angle of her head evokes the Pre-Raphaelite pictures by D. G. Rossetti. Around her middle is the famous 'Boy Toy' belt which she wore to the awards. 1985 was certainly Madonna's year. On the back of the album she played concerts in the US, opening in Seattle on 10 April, and selling 17,000 odd tickets for three nights at the Radio City Music Hall. While 'Dress You Up' was in the top 5 in the US charts, 'Crazy For You', 'Holiday' and 'Into the Groove' all featured in the UK top 20, a pretty impressive feat for a newcomer.

MATERIAL GIRL
(Peter Brown/Robert Rans)

BACKED WITH 'Pretender' this was another hit single, and drew comparisons with Cyndi Lauper both because of the shrill voice Madonna sings it in and perhaps also because of the sentiment of the lyric. The phrase "material world" which occurs in the lyric, cropped up from time to time in an early Eighties song by The Police. In that tune, Sting's lyric portrays humanity as spirits in the material world. Madonna's song identifies with materialism. What she wants is money, clothes, the good life, and men... preferably able to supply those things. There is also a small cross-reference here to The Miracles's 1960 Tamla hit 'Shop Around'. Relationships are presented in terms of capitalism as commodities, and playing the field becomes akin to trading stocks and shares.

The music is formula Madonna, with synth figures all over it and a strong backbeat. A robotic male voice repeats the hook just in case you didn't get the general Brave New World yuppie vibe. The video gave her a chance to express some of her admiration for Marilyn Monroe by imitating a scene from Monroe's film *Gentlemen Prefer Blondes*, in which the Fifties screen goddess had sung 'Diamonds Are A Girl's Best Friend'. This of course fitted very neatly with the lyrics for 'Material Girl', which Madonna duly sang while wearing a pink satin ankle-length dress, evening gloves and diamond bracelets. The Monroe comparisons went on for quite a while, fuelled by Madonna's determination to have a film career alongside her music. But it has become abundantly obvious that she is a tougher cookie than Monroe, more focused and in control than Norma Jean ever was.

Some commentators will have you believe that 'Material Girl' is ironic, a pungent satire on the

Reagan/Thatcher young-guns-go-for-it era. Which just goes to show that pop music and irony don't mix. In 1996 this was the song Madonna said she would never sing again if she could help it. We're with you on that one, Maddy.

ANGEL
(Madonna/Steve Bray)

THIS STARTS with a laugh and an echo panned left and right. The song is built on a three chord ascending hook which serves for the verse and the chorus. The lyric is a bit of a one mouthful meringue, and The machine-like feel is exacerbated by the constant 8th rhythms throughout. The angel image is repeated and vocal harmonies add just a little sprinkle of fairy dust. It's effectively a two-bar phrase that doesn't go anywhere, but merely peters out. This is a song that is less even than the sum of its parts.

LIKE A VIRGIN
(Billy Steinberg/Tom Kelly)

NOW THIS was clever. Here is an intro that manages to throw not one but two hooks at its defenceless audience, taking two stalwart pop clichés and serving them up for a new era. The bass-line on the intro is a re-working of the kind of three-note bass motif that originally propelled the Four Tops' 'I Can't Help Myself' to the top of the charts in 1965 and periodically still

gets nicked in order for other acts to joyride their Motown pastiches to the stars. On the other side of the mix is a chordal stab which is taken from Chuck Berry. Madonna puts her little girl lost voice on top of this unholy stew, while at the bottom Tony Thompson wacks the drums, giving the track far more whallop than a drum machine ever could. The bass line is also doubled by synth.

Madonna later said of the song, "I like innuendo, I like irony, I like the way things can be taken on different levels", a statement which highlights the ambiguity of the song. The lyric is hung on the frisky ambiguity of the word "like". She may be like a virgin but is she one? This lyric really covered all the bases. The real virgins out there could sing the song and clutch it to their hearts in anticipation of the Main Event, or to encourage themselves to hold off for a bit longer. The more experienced girls could fantasise about how going with this guy was going to make it all seem like the first time all over again. And as for the boys... well here was a maiden making them feel they would annihilate her previous sexual history as soon as they got her in their clinches. Clever. Mind you, this version is nothing compared to the live one Madonna featured in concert in 1990, where the track is slowed into a sleazy bump'n'grind – which was always the sticky heart of this particular cupcake. 'Heart Of Gold' it ain't.

Somewhat naively, Madonna commented, "I was surprised with

how people reacted to 'Like A Virgin' because when I did the song, to me, I was singing about how something made me feel a certain way – brand-new and fresh – and everyone interpreted it as I don't want to be a virgin anymore. Fuck my brains out! That's not what I sang at all." Interestingly enough, it's not what Billy Steinberg meant, either, when he wrote it. Steinberg told the *LA Times*, "The idea for that song came from personal experience. I wasn't just trying to somehow get that racy word "virgin" in a lyric. I was saying... that I may not really be a virgin – I've been battered romantically and emotionally like many people – but I'm starting a new relationship and it just feels so good, it's healing all the wounds and making me feel like I've never done this before."

The single was helped by the success of the video shot in Venice.

Initially, Nile Rogers wasn't at all convinced by this song, but had to change his mind when the hook embedded itself in his brain. After the appropriate surgery, he told the *LA Times*, "I liked the melody a lot, because the tune was catchy, but I didn't think that the lyric "like a virgin" was such a terrific hook. It just didn't seem like, you know, the all-time catch-phrase. But after about four days I couldn't get the song out of my head, and I said, 'You know, Madonna, I really apologise, because if it's so catchy it stayed in my head for four days, it must be something.'" If a seasoned pro like Rogers was vulnerable, what chance did the rest us have?!

OVER AND OVER
(Madonna/Steve Bray)

A SONG THAT lives down to its title. Horrible sounding drums, synths a-go-go, and a three-chord trick pushed over the edge as Madonna sings a story about determination, about picking yourself up from disappointments. The production is sparse, you get a few echoes on the voice, there's a silky chorused guitar from Rogers and the thin sound has dated badly. Not something you'd want to play over and over.

LOVE DON'T LIVE HERE ANYMORE
(Miles Gregory)

A HIT FOR Rose Royce in 1978 and Jimmy Nail in 1985, this was the most ambitious track which the gal from Detroit had attempted so far, included to give the album a little more sophistication and show that she was capable of far more than just the shrill disco beat. The first part of the song is carried without drums, instead acoustic guitar and synth strings provide the platform from which Madonna tries to get to grips with the emotional demands of the song. She certainly manages to pull more tone out of her voice than ever before on record, sounding occasionally like a higher-pitched Alison Moyet, but the deeper resonance of the tune eludes her. When Thompson enters on drums, he drives the rhythm along just a touch too emphatically. Ironically, this is one of those tracks where a drum machine might have been better. Toward the end Madonna's attempts to emote like a soul singer don't really work and the gasp at the end doesn't ring true. However, the effort deserves a commendation for bravery and was a sign that she was going to set herself challenges. It gained a further surprising lease of life on the *Something To Remember* collection.

INTO THE GROOVE
(Madonna/Steve Bray)

THIS TRACK reached a huge audience via its inclusion on the soundtrack of *Desperately Seeking Susan*, a light-hearted comedy in which Rosanna Arquette had the limelight stolen from her by Madonna, since Madonna's character really only required her to be herself. 'Into The Groove' was added to this album later to enhance sales after it had been a hit single, with 'Shoo-Bee-Doo'on the B-side.

Drums and synth bass lines burst straight in, and after a few spoken lines, Madonna is into the first chorus. Her voice is double-tracked and given a typically trebly quality, and the synth line that counterpoints the tune really adds something. Good as the track is, it would have been better if Thompson had been on this. The bridge ("live out your fantasy here with me") has a delicious harmony

in which Madonna adds a low register voice to the main one. As her career has progressed she's learned to make effective use of the lower part of her voice. The lyrics are a simple invitation to dance but carrying a sexual undertone. As with 'Like A Virgin', there was a lyric hook for all the shy girls:"At night I lock the door so no-one else can see". It suggested this material girl might not be quite as brazen as her gum-chewing image.

Madonna now thinks of it as 'dorky':"When I was writing it, I was sitting in a fourth-floor walk-up on Avenue B, and there was this gorgeous Puerto Rican boy sitting across from me that I wanted to go out on a date with, and I just wanted to get it over with." Did she get the boy? Will you get the boy, or the girl, next time you're on the edge of a dance floor? 'Into The Groove' will make you feel like you're a winner either way. And that's one of the best things pop music can do for ya. Madonna's first great single.

DRESS YOU UP
(Peggy Stanziale/Andrea LaRusso)

IT WAS the lyrics on this tune that hit the button more than anything. The backing was a typical drum-machine driven dance track with a two-chord verse and a chorus approached by a churchy suspension which resolved into a four chord turnaround lit up by a single-note stuttering guitar line courtesy of Nile Rogers. The bridge even had a rock guitar solo and toward the end, the drums get thinned out to give a breath of sweaty air before the dancing recommences. But the words ... ah! Here was love as High Fashion and the lover as Dress Model. The catwalk and the bedroom suddenly collided: "Gonna dress you up in my love/All over your body". Where else?

And with what? She was a material girl in more than one sense. Another infuriating hook that buried itself in your consciousness. On the flip of the single you'll find 'I Know It'.

SHOO-BEE-DOO
(Madonna)

THIS SLICE of high calorie dessert comes as a welcome respite from the machine drumming and blurting synths, with a slow introduction where Madonna sings over a piano and strings. The song has a reasonable tune and clearly looks back to the genre of doo-wop and early Sixties girl groups like The Shirelles or The Crystals or The Ronettes. The throw-away lyrics treat of relationship problems but in this respect should be compared with 'Till Death Us Do Part' which is far more convincing. A sax break by Lenny Pickett is the cherry on the top of this after-dinner treat. The lyric clichés on the coda are nicely phrased by Madonna.

PRETENDER
(Madonna/Steve Bray)

THIS IS probably one of the weakest songs on the album, sounding like a slowed-down 'Into The Groove', starting with a chorus and then moving to a verse. The lyric talks about a guy who isn't what he seems to be. It's a tale of seduction, of things happening too quickly, of the insecurity the woman feels in this situation, and as such would surely strike a note with the teenagers in her audience. Musically, it never gets going.

STAY
(Madonna/Steve Bray)

ANOTHER weak track using a fast triple rhythm with synths going about their usual business and Madonna being double-tracked, with a quick run round a three chord sequence on the chorus. Notable highlights (such as they are) include a noise like someone slapping a microphone and a spoken sequence toward the end. The song runs its unwavering course with no dynamics to the finish, where it would seem in a fit of desperation Madonna tries to get in some scat singing. A dull end with two tracks that became B-sides to an album that is sparky in parts.

True Blue

Original UK issue: Sire WX 54; CD 925442-2, July 1986.

THE **DIFFICULT THIRD ALBUM. MADONNA STARTED WORK ON** *TRUE BLUE* **IN THE** autumn of 1985 and decided to co-produce it Steve Bray and Patrick Leonard. In addition, she co-wrote all but one of the songs with Bray and Leonard, the latter destined to become a vital partner in her musical odyssey. During these sessions a song called 'Spotlight' was recorded but held over to a future release. The album carried the dedication, "to my husband, the coolest guy in the universe", referring to actor Sean Penn, whom Madonna had married in August 1985 in a blaze of publicity. The cover photo and the video for the opening song showed a change of image for Madonna. She was no longer the Boy Toy. Instead she had opted for a more sophisticated Fifties look. She called the record her most personal album to date.

Long-time friend and collaborator Bray commented, "She was very much in love. It was obvious... if she's in love she'll write love songs. If she's not in love she definitely won't be writing love songs. That's why the long songs we recorded aren't on the LP – she didn't feel that they were real enough for her at the time." By 1991 this album had sold 17 million copies. It was the top-selling album of 1986, going number 1 in Australia, Austria, Belgium, Brazil, Canada, Denmark, Finland, France, Germany, Hong Kong, Ireland, Israel, Italy, Japan, The Netherlands, New Zealand, Norway, the Phillipines, Switzerland, the UK and Venezuela. True Blue consolidated Madonna's position as the world's biggest new pop act.

PAPA DON'T PREACH
(Brian Elliot. Additional lyrics by Madonna)

ANUMBER 1 single in the US, backed with 'Ain't No Big Deal', 'Papa Don't Preach' was a single that got Madonna into more controversy as it tackled the subject of teenage pregnancy. Conservatives in the US who had previously hated everything Madonna stood for unexpectedly found themselves supporting the song because they thought it was anti-abortion. She herself said it was "a message song that everyone is going to take the wrong way. Immediately they're going to say I am advising every young girl to go out and get pregnant. When I first heard the song I thought it was silly. But then I thought, wait a minute, this song is really about a girl who is making a decision in her life." The string introduction was devised by keyboardist Fred Zarr, a friend of Mark Kamins, who improvised it on an Emulator II synth. Originally it didn't have an introduction but Madonna liked it so much that they kept it. An orchestral introduction sets the mood before the drums enter.

The lyric was the best that had yet appeared on a Madonna record. In it, a daughter approaches her father with the unwelcome news that she's expecting a baby. The verse has two parts. In the chorus it seems that she is making the decision to keep the child and rejects her father's moralising. The lyric skilfully picks out a number of aspects of the situation from the father's attitude to abortion to early marriage, to the boy's offer to marry her, and the imminent loss of freedom that maternity will bring. The chorus is punchy enough, and there's a pleasant acoustic guitar solo, but as a whole the song seems musically a trifle under-powered.

All too frequently pop music deals with wishes and dreams instead of consequences, and this song stands out for that reason. Here at least Madonna provoked controversy to a useful end.

Songwriter Brian Elliot arranged to go to the studio when Madonna wasn't there to hear what was being done with the song. He recalled how listening to it for the first time, a voice behind him said, "Well, did I wreck your song?" "I turned around and there she was... We had a spirited discussion at that point about certain interpretations of lines, and it was resolved to the mutual delight of all concerned."

OPEN YOUR HEART
(Madonna/Gardner Cole/Peter Ralfelson)

THIS IS punchier and more upbeat, opening with a cry of "watch out!". Over a continuous percussive battery and through another two-part verse, the song unfolds a tale of an unrequited love for someone seen on a street through some very predictable rhymes and lock/key imagery. The chorus could be Belinda Carlisle. This was originally written with Cyndi Lauper in mind, and The Temptations also considered recording it. Songwriters Cole and Ralfelson spent a year trying to perfect the song. Ralfelson commented, "Madonna redid some of the lyric ideas, and (with) Patrick Leonard, changed the arrangement around. Pat and her put a bass line underneath the song and got it into a rock'n'roll dance area instead of just rock'n'roll. The original was more rock/pop than dance."

Of the video, Madonna said "It was about innocence versus decadence really, and in the end I chose innocence. I mean, that's what the child represented - the child-like quality everybody has versus all the people in the club who were jaded and decadent and depraved." Call it undistinguished. The single went to number 4 in the US with 'Lucky Star' on the flip.

WHITE HEAT
(Madonna/Pat Leonard)

THIS IS dedicated to the actor Jimmy Cagney and named after his film of 1949 about psychotic gangster Cody Jarrett who dies when the huge gasoline tank he is standing on explodes. There are two quotations from the original soundtrack of 'White Heat', one at the beginning and another toward the end, with speech and gunshots. Madonna adds to the general air of detective reference by quoting Clint Eastwood's famous "make my day" catchphrase. As a comparison to how aural quotes from film soundtracks can be used to create a sense of drama on a track, cross-refer to Kate Bush's 'Hounds of Love' and the Siouxsie & The Banshees track '92 Degrees' from *Tinderbox*. The song itself is a standard up tempo dance track with synth bass and double-tracked vocals, supported by male voices on the chorus. The drum machine's tone and unvarying regularity help to give this a somewhat sterile feeling. It should also be compared with some parts of the *Dick Tracy* soundtrack. Used as the B-side of *Who's That Girl* in 1987.

LIVE TO TELL
(Madonna/Pat Leonard)

THIS WAS the theme song for Sean Penn's film *At Close .ange*. Here Madonna bravely tackled another serious theme, that of child abuse,

although the lyric is couched in such a way that listeners may interpret the general theme more broadly. It certainly isn't as direct as Suzanne Vega's 'Luka'. Anyone who has lived through a difficult time which they want to keep to themselves would be able to project their feelings onto this number. A sustained single note leads into a wash of synth strings and electric piano number There are two interlocking motifs, while the snare drum is a little too loud and to the front of the mix. A touch of Heavy Metal guitar strains at the leash in the background (groowwll!) but is never let out of the kennel. It has to be said that the music fails to live up to the lyric's intent. If you took Madonna's vocal off this it could be anyone. Toward the end the music breaks down and returns to the intro creating a sense of suspense. The secret is never revealed.

It's a more thoughtful vocal from Madonna. According to Pat Leonard, Madonna wrote the words on the spot and sang a single take onto a demo: "She sang it only once (for the demo) and that was the vocal we used because it was so innocent and so shy. She had a legal pad in her hand... and you can hear the paper. It's as naive, as raw, as can be and that's part of what gave it all its charm." The music was written for a film but the film people turned it down. When Madonna wrote the words: "I thought about my relationship with my parents and the lying that went on". The song is about "being strong, and questioning whether you can be that strong but ultimately surviving." In 1995 Madonna said this was her favourite of her songs, because "it sums up all of my yearning and a lot of my pain, really". Along with 'Papa Don't Preach', this is the album's strongest track.

WHERE'S THE PARTY
(Madonna/Steve Bray/Pat Leonard)

SIDE 2 of the vinyl version kicks off with this dance track, a standard Madonna arrangement with drum machine, synth, clattering rhythm, and quite an empty mix. Not really for listening to too closely. If you want to dance, stick this on and let Madonna's words wash over you. The lyric makes it clear that 'week' is a four-letter word, as is 'work'. The weekend is for partying, so get on down! Madonna said of this song, "It's my ultimate statement about what it's like to be in the middle of this Press stuff with everybody on my back, my world about to cave in. Whenever I feel like that – and it does get to me sometimes – I say 'Wait a minute, I'm supposed to be having a good time here, so where's the party?' It doesn't have to be this way. I can still enjoy my life."

TRUE BLUE
(Madonna/Stephen Bray)

THIS WAS a love song for Sean, written again in homage to early Sixties girl group pop. Apparently it's based on a favourite saying of his. The track is in a fast compound time and makes extensive use of the king of all doo-wop chord sequences, what is known in the business as the I-VI-IV-V sequence (B G♯ minor E F♯ in the key of B major). This is like a saccharine up tempo version of 'Shoo-Bee-Doo' with telegraphed rhymes. Not surprisingly, it was a hit. The only real moment of interest is when the vocal introduces a bass countermelody on the second chorus. A song that is merely cute and not really up to being the title track of an album. It was released as a single with 'Holiday' on the B-side, including in an extended dance format.

LA ISLA BONITA
(Madonna/Pat Leonard/
Bruce Gaitsch)

MADONNA plays record markets the way Meryl Streep does accents. Rule 1 of being a massively successful recording artist: reach as many ethnic groups as you can. This came out as a single in 1987 with an 'instrumental edit' on the reverse. 'La Isla Bonita' was Madonna's first love-missile aimed at Hispanic listeners, many of whom would probably have cheerfully lobbed it back with a warhead packed with classic recordings of de Falla, Rodriguez, Albanez, and Paco de Pena. The song was originally a lament for a mythical Spanish island called San Pedro and was offered initially to Michael Jackson, who turned it down,

Madonna took the single to a US number 4. The conga-littered intro ushers us quicker than the sweep of a flamenco dancer's skirt and the click of castanets, into Madonna's tale of balmy (and barmy) romance on the good isle, as the title translates. Right on cue we get a minor key chorus, and following it some phrases from page 17 of Manuel DePlonka's 'Spanish-guitar-play-in-a-day'. Percussion comes courtesy of Paulinho da Costa, who presumably knew what he was letting himself in for. Madonna described this as "a tribute to the beauty and mystery of Latin American people". This is one of those songs where you just know the video is going to be marginally more interesting. But on a cold wet afternoon in the city, hey! A little escapism, y'all!

JIMMY JIMMY
(Madonna/Steve Bray)

ACCORDING to Madonna: "I used to fantasise that we grew up in the same neighbourhood and that he [Jimmy Dean] moved away and became a big star." This is the sorry tale of a young male who smashes his car up and says he'll be King of Las Vegas. Your assignment for this one is to find how important the name Jimmy is to the history of pop. Jimmy Mack, James Dean...rock on.

Is he the leader of the pack reincarnated? The harmony vocals certainly cast a backward allusion to early Sixties pop... but not much. Commentators who draw entirely erroneous comparisons with the wayward Mr Penn will be asked to get their coats and exit. In the lyric he leaves before she can tell him how much she luurves him. He, of course, is also a part of her character. 'Oop shoo boop oop oop sha la la', goes the refrain in teenage code. The antidote for this track is the Beach Boys' 'Don't Worry Baby', an incomparably more profound and more musical story of what happens to young men who insist on proving their virility by racing cars. Used as the B-side of 'Causing A Commotion'.

LOVE MAKES THE WORLD GO ROUND
(Madonna/Pat Leonard)

SUNG BY Madonna during her stand at Live Aid. An upbeat track to close the album using Latin American sounding drums, the Latin feel reinforced by samba synth brass touches. The lyrics are anti-war and anti-poverty and certainly have their heart in the right place, though they have trouble finding an adequate musical setting. The sentiment about not making easy judgements neatly links back up with 'Papa Don't Preach'. Paulinho da Costa gets to add some real percussion just to humanise things a bit. The middle eight is sparse in terms of instrumentation. An average way of ending True Blue.

You Can Dance

Sire WX 76; CD 925535-2, released September 1987

"I hate it when people do mastermixes of my records. I don't want to hear my songs changed like that."

YOU CAN DANCE WAS MADONNA'S FIRST RETROSPECTIVE AND IT WAS AIMED blatantly at the dance segment of her audience. It was a record designed to be danced to at parties and not to be listened to. It came in a bright red sleeve on which Madonna appeared with short blonde hair, dressed like a Spanish matador, and had a free poster. The gold wrap-around sleeve note by Brian Chin explained that for this release 7 of her songs had been taken back into the studio and subjected to the process known as re-mixing. At this point, it's pretty essential that we call time-out and explain for the uninitiated what exactly 'mixing' and 're-mixing' are.

There are a number of distinct stages to making a record. First, all the musical parts are recorded on multi-track tape or digitally onto hard disk or some such system. This means that at the end of the recording there are usually many parts to a song. There may be several lead vocals, backing vocals, a guitar, a bass, a number of synth parts and sound effects and a drum machine, itself occupying more than one track. Put simply, Mixing is the process of deciding how loud these are going to be in relation to each other and what particular sound effects will be added to each instrument, and also where in the stereo 'field' each instrument is going to be placed: left or right or centre.

Improvements in studio technology have meant that the possibilities for shaping the sound after it has been recorded are almost limitless. For example, the arrangement itself can be created at the mixing stage. When you are listening to Madonna tracks such as the ones on You Can Dance, if you hear an instrument disappear it isn't because the player stopped playing at that bar or the drums were programmed not to have a snare and kick drum at that point, it's because during the mixing process the fader (the volume control on that track) was simply pulled down, and then pushed up again when the instrument comes back in. Digital technology has also made it possible to 'sample' various sounds and then loop them so that they repeat at a particular frequency. A particular vocal phrase can be endlessly copied, repeated, chopped up, transposed up or down in pitch and given more echo or reverb or treble or bass or whatever.

Mixing is an interpretative process, which the artist is usually involved with, but which is generally looked after by the producer. For example, how loud should the drums be? How much should the vocals stand out? These are creative decisions which will change the finished piece of music. However, without some music to work from, the mixer has nothing. It is an example of secondary creativity. Dance music elevates the DJ and the mixer to being almost on a level with the musician. In my opinion this is false. Manipulation of pre-recorded sound sources may be creative in a secondary sense, and may be valid in its own field, but it is pseudo-musicianship.

From the record companies point of view, the rise of the re-mix has been a commercial boon because it means making more money out of the same piece of music. Instead of going into the studio and recording two or three tracks for a single, very often the same piece of music can be replicated on a disc with several different mixes. Madonna's later singles have frequently been subjected to endless remixing. This has meant that unlike the works of many other artists, Madonna's singles have been especially uninteresting from the point of view of being a source of new material on their B-sides. Her B sides tend to be either album tracks or endless remixes of the A side.

The mixes on *You Can Dance* exhibit a number of typical mixing techniques. Instrumental passages are lengthened to increase the time for dancing, which undermines the tighter structure of the pop song. Vocal phrases are repeated, subjected to multiple echo, panned across the stereo image, or sampled and then played rhythmically. At certain points almost nothing is left in the mix except the drums and at others the drums are removed with only the high-hat left to keep time. Approximate running times are given to indicate the difference between the length of the re-mix and the original track.

Safe usage of *You Can Dance* requires that you keep moving for the duration of the record. Do not under any circumstances attempt to listen to this record whilst maintaining a static position or wearing headphones with your eyes shut. Failure to heed this warning could lead to boredom, insanity and hospitalisation. The publishers and yours truly cannot be held responsible etc, etc! In the event of accidental exposure, keep the patient in silence with a hot drink until emergency rescue services arrive from your nearest music store. The prescription is *Pet Sounds*, taken aurally, twice a day for a week.

SPOTLIGHT
(Madonna/Steve Bray/C. Hudson)
6:24

THIS SONG was held over from Madonna's early albums and here is mixed by 'Jellybean' Benitez. It has a noticeable resemblance to the chord sequence of 'Holiday', which may account for its earlier rejection. The music is carried by the usual arrangement of drums, bass synth and other higher synth parts. The lyric runs through the usual everyone-is-a-star schtick. Remember: if you want to be famous, sing about it and reality may catch up. Along the way we get a brief harmony vocal, vocal echo, a piano section and some violin phrases. Without any problem at all 'Spotlight' segues straight into the next number.

HOLIDAY
(C. Hudson/L. Stevens)
6:32 / Original 6:08

ACCORDING to the sleeve note this mix is the one Benitez always wanted to do with the track. "There are new sounds on the 1987 remix," he notes, "but it had a groove that needed no improvement." It certainly has a clearer overall sound than the original release, the guitar part seems more to the front, and otherwise we get a piano break and a middle section with drums, echoed voice and little else. If you thought the original version was numbing, try this. It could render novacaine obsolete. I've had teeth out with less.

EVERYBODY
(Madonna) 6:31 / Original 4:57

THIS WAS Madonna's first single, produced by Mark Kamins. This mix starts with four repetitions of the vocal hook and then moves into a stark rhythm-centred arrangement. As expected, the middle section features the standard 'beat-break' and a skeletal synth tune. Games are played with the word 'dance', which is echoed and slowed-down. The rhythm of this track is especially stiff and the extended length merely emphasises it. At the very end the drums are pulled out, leaving Madonna repeating the "get up and do your thing" phrase which hovers over the intro to the next song.

PHYSICAL ATTRACTION
(R. Lucas)

THIS IS the same length as the original cut (6:35). The mix of this version seems clearer, with the guitar line more up front. It follows the original until the middle eight where the arrangement is then varied. Overall, the empty arrangement does little to hide the paucity of ideas in the song. Those of you with the vinyl version of 'You Can Dance' will notice a strange, disconcerting sound at the end of this track. It is called silence. It means you must turn over the platter to cavort once more.

OVER AND OVER
(Madonna / Steve Bray)
7:09 / Original 4:09

THE REMIX session for 'Over and Over' was "notable for its energy", recalls Steve Thompson, who redid the cut with his partner, engineer Michael Barbiero. Keyboard tracks played by Jack Waldman and percussion by Jimmy Maelen were added to the original Nile Rodgers production. Ultimately, the game plan here was to add fresh ideas while maintaining the integrity of the song and artist - but in this case especially, "There was a lot of intensity", says Thompson. "Jimmy really wailed playing live percussion to a drum machine track." There are a lot of rhythm–only sections in this version which almost doubles the length of the song, making it live up to its title even more. A couple of the vocal phrases sound like Enya being mugged in a Euro disco.

INTO THE GROOVE
(Madonna / S. Bray)
8:15 / 4:40

REMIXED with 'generous overdubs' by Shep Pettibone, this is another marathon version. Much of the attention is grabbed at the outset by the sampling of Madonna's phrase "c'mon", which is then triggered in such a way that the "c"

sound becomes percussively repeated. Ah, the wonders of digital technology. Or not. The first verse doesn't get started until about 90 seconds in. After the first "Now I know you're mine" there's a fairly drastic percussion break with a lot of sampled sound and repetition of phrases like "step to the beat" and "c'mon". The last verse puts plenty of echo on the vocals, causing some overlap on the phrases. There's also a touch of Bruce Hornsby-like pianumber. The track closes with congas, whistles and timbale giving the song a Mexican ending. Hey! Jose!!....

WHERE'S THE PARTY?
(Madonna / S. Bray / Pat Leonard)
7:06 / 4:20

THIS IS musically one of the least uninteresting tracks if only for the fact that the arrangement is thicker. Clumps of male voices shout back the hook from the outset and other highlights include congas, a sampled vocal phrase, cackling laughter and some hideous electronic handclaps. The ending is exceptionally repetitious. Empires rise and fall, the ice-caps swell and retreat, nations migrate, comets come and go and return... and she's still singing that damned hook!

Like A Prayer

Sire WX239; CD 925844-2; March 1989

1988 HAD BEEN A QUIET YEAR FOR **MADONNA** ON THE RECORDING FRONT. Following the lack of success for the film *Who's That Girl*, she went into theatre, acting in a Broadway production *Speed The Plough*. This was not a happy experience and caused her much frustration and depression. The critical reviews were not favourable. Her marriage with Sean Penn went from one disaster to the next. Eventually she decided the relationship was irretrievable. This culminated in her filing for divorce in January 1989. Like many other artists, it was from this personal turmoil Madonna created her best album to date. She had turned thirty, the same age her mother was when she died.

Her next album was to be cathartic. As she put it, "Everybody wants to know about everything I do, so I might as well confront it in my work."

Like A Prayer moved Madonna beyond the confines of dance/disco music. The songs are more directly autobiographical than before, as she deals with various experiences of childhood, her relationship with her father, with her dead mother, and with Catholicism. She said, "My first couple of albums I would say came from the little girl in me, who is interested only in having people like me, in being entertaining and charming and frivolous and sweet. And this new one is the adult side of me, which is concerned with being brutally honest." In 1991 she told Rolling Stone, "I've written my best things when I'm upset, but then who hasn't? What's the point of sitting down and notating your happiness?" Elsewhere she said, "In the past my records tended to be a reflection of current influences. This album is more about past musical experiences. The songs 'Keep It Together' and 'Express Yourself' for instance are sort of my tributes to Sly and the Family Stone. 'Oh Father' is my tribute to Simon and Garfunkel, whom I loved. Also the overall emotional content of the album is drawn from what I was going through when I was growing up."

She also gave an insight into her methods of working: "Lots of times Pat Leonard will come up with a piece of music like 'Oh Father' – we did very little to change it musically – he throws the music at me and I just listen to it over and over again. And somehow the music suggests words to me and I just start writing words down. Other times I will come to Pat with an idea for a song, either lyrically or emotionally and say, 'Let's do something like this' or I'll have a melody line in my head which I will sing to him and he will sort of pound out the chords. It takes a lot longer to do it that way because I don't play an instrument but ultimately it's a lot more personal."

It is said that the album was made with more live musicians and used a greater proportion of live first takes. Pat Leonard revealed that the songs 'Like A Prayer', 'Spanish Eyes', 'Till Death Us Do Part', 'Dear Jessie', 'Promise To Try' and 'Cherish' were written in just a few weeks. Two other songs written with Steve Bray, 'First Is A Kiss' and 'Love Attack' were rejected because they didn't fit in with the confessional tone of the album.

Musically it remains the most engaging, listenable album to carry her name. The album bore the inscription, "this album is dedicated to my mother who taught me how to pray". So much for the notion that this represents some sort of final reckoning with her religion. At the very least the album demonstrates the ambivalence she felt about Catholicism. She told the *New York Times* how as a theme, Catholicism "runs rampant through my album. It's me struggling with the mystery and magic that surrounds it." Years later she commented, "I love the rituals, particularly of Catholicism, and the architecture of great, beautiful churches and the mysteriousness of it all... I've always known that Catholicism is a completely sexist, repressed sin-and-punishment-based religion." To record it she called on the talents of a large number of musicians, whilst collaborating with Pat Leonard and Steve Bray. Leonard said, "all her emotion poured out of her when she was recording [it]. We called it her divorce album... Normally she's a very fast worker, but it took maybe three or four times as long to make the record because she kept breaking down. But she kept going."

The album sleeve presented a close-up of her midriff, her jeans and various items of jewellery, something of a throwback to her earlier material girl image, and clearly alluded to the cover of the Rolling Stones' *Sticky Fingers* (1971). Initial runs of the vinyl pressing had patchouli oil mixed into the glue to make it a more sensual experience. Big critical claims have been made for this record. *Rolling Stone*'s reviewer opined it was "proof that not only that Madonna should be taken seriously as an artist, but that hers is one of the most compelling voices of the Eighties." By the Nineties it had sold 11 million copies. Aside from *The Immaculate Collection*, this is the one album of Madonna's which merits being considered in any list of Albums-of-the-Eighties.

LIKE A PRAYER
(Madonna/Pat Leonard)

A FEW SECONDS of heavy rock guitar are suddenly cut off and replaced by choir and organ announcing the main theme of the song. Then the drums kick in to a typically clattery rhythm track as Madonna tackles the first chorus. It becomes apparent this is not going to be a straight dance track when the percussion gets pulled out for another section before returning for the second chorus. The guitars flicker silky left and right with a bubbling sequenced bass line. It's an effective chorus. The lyrics are ambiguous - who is she talking to? Her father? God? A lover?

Rule number two of mainstream pop is that if you want to tackle religion make sure people can think it's a love song (see U2). The chart success was helped by a controversial video featuring Madonna with a black Jesus, stigmata, burning crosses and so on. What did it all mean? Having 'Act Of Contrition' on the B-side certainly wouldn't have helped people who had the single.

Musically, this was one of the most complex tracks she'd ever recorded. The percussive rhythm is interrupted, creating a great sense of tension. Madonna's voice is supported by gospel choir-type backing vocals, and a short break with one of the singers wordlessly emoting. It topped the charts in 30 countries. 'Like A Prayer' has a great sense of drama and building atmosphere. The early ingredients of her sound are still there but given a much richer overlay of sound. This was written in a day with Leonard "about the influence of Catholicism on my life and the passion it provokes in me... I don't make fun of Catholicism. I deeply respect Catholicism, its mystery, and fear, and oppressiveness, its passion, and its discipline, and its obsession with guilt."

EXPRESS YOURSELF
(Madonna/Steve Bray)

THIS WAS the second hit single from the album, backed by 'The Look Of Love'. A typical upbeat number with Madonna exhorting the women in her audience not to go for second-best, to express their feelings, and get their men to express theirs. Feminists would certainly have a quarrel with the idea that all women want to feel emotionally pampered by having themselves put on a throne. Here Madonna dismisses the satin sheets and gold baubles of material success. If it doesn't work, then you're better off on your own, she says, quite possibly expressing some personal feelings. There's a much thicker vocal texture almost all the way through and a brass break for the middle. As she told the *New York Times*, "The message of the song is that people should always say what it is they want". She also says that "The ultimate thing behind the song is that if you don't express yourself, if you don't say what you want, then you're not going to get it. And in effect you are chained down by your inability to say what you feel or go after what you want."

"No matter how in control you think you are about sexuality in a relationship there is always the power struggle... always a certain amount of compromise. Of being beholden, if you love them. You do it because you choose to. No one put the chain around this neck but me. I

Madonna Louise Veronica Ciccone, in 1985.

The 1983 visit to London – when no-one knew who she was.

Madonna at the 1984 MTV Awards, in her 'Boy Toy' wedding gown.

Madonna removes her Keith Haring outfit during an early performance of 'Like A Virgin'.

Like A Virgin (1984).

On stage at the Philadelphia Live Aid concert, July 13, 1985.

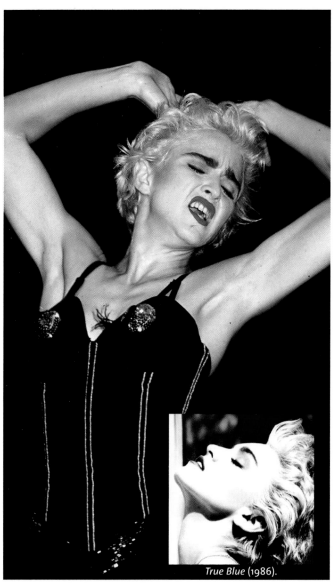

True Blue (1986).

On stage during the 'Who's That Girl' tour, 1987.

Above and below, right: the 'Who's That Girl' tour.

Like A Prayer (1989).

Dick Tracy (1990).

Above and top right: Madonna on her 'Blonde Ambition' tour in 1990.

The conical bra was a hallmark of Madonna 'Blonde Ambition' tour.

was chained to my desire." The video for this number was based on Fritz Lang's 1926 film *Metropolis*.

LOVE SONG
(Madonna/Prince)

OR, A collaboration made in heaven? The two pint-sized megastars first met in 1985. Three years later they considered writing a musical, worked on several songs together but nothing came of it. Prince salvaged a rough mix of one of these and gave it to her. They then worked on it, sending the tapes back and forth. The imaginatively-titled 'Love Song' starts with Madonna asking in French, "I am ready, are you ready?" The idiosyncratic arrangement assembled from lots of little bits give away Prince's hand in the track. He supplies flickers of Jimmy Nolan funk guitar, and falsetto vocals, singing in both his upper and lower register with a laconic grace. At times the track's melody is reminiscent of some of The Temptations cuts with Eddie Kendricks on vocals. It certainly brings out a very different quality in Madonna's voice. Madonna puts in a couple more Detroit French phrases toward the end before the track fades away with her singing a few edgier phrases. A lazy, sexy mutha.

TILL DEATH US DO PART
(Madonna/Pat Leonard)

DESPITE the breezy synth backing and fast tempo, this track boasts a memorable chorus and a plangent verse as Madonna charts the twists and turns of a slowly failing relationship. It starts with some guitar playing with an echo delay sending the notes out in the style pioneered by the Edge of U2. The chorus is a fast turnaround with a poignant melody over its minor chords. It expresses the conflict of being with someone who doesn't love themselves and doesn't love her and is threatening violence. The nightmare is created by the continual onrush and the sequence where Madonna speaks and sings the same lines about broken doors. She doesn't even have the consolation of knowing that he's in love with someone else, and he won't change. 'Till Death Us Do Part' has an appropriately claustrophobic carousel of a whirl. It ends with a wah-wah guitar lick and a broken bottle. And a marriage in ruins.

PROMISE TO TRY
(Madonna/Pat Leonard)

A SOMBRE, moody piano introduction ushers in this ballad in which Madonna addresses herself as a child after her mother's death. The chord sequence is marred only by the premature return to the key chord at the end of the first two phrases. The piano is supported by strings and the overall effect is slightly reminiscent of Elton John. The bridge wanders into different tonal territory, and a cello solo. It's a predictable arrangement but a good one. The song is brought to a low-key and appropriately short ending. Madonna resists the temptation to barnstorm a grand finale. It ain't over till the thin lady sings. A controlled performance. It would be interesting to hear Tori Amos do this. If she'd written it, it would probably be a more angular and better song; but if she covered it she'd probably be unable to resist making it too theatrical. Understatement is not a word one readily associates with Madonna the Queen of Excess, but here, for once, she makes it. As she once said, "One of the hardest things I've faced in my life was the death of my mother and that's something I really haven't gotten over to this day". She also said, "It was the single most... the greatest event in my life. What happened when I was six years old, changed forever how I am. I can't describe in words the effect it had. I became an over-achiever to get approval from the world".

CHERISH
(Madonna/Pat Leonard)

SIDE TWO of the tape and vinyl versions picks up the mood with this wonderfully sunny, romantic love song. It has been said that this owes something to an Associations

record of 1960 of the same name. A fast dancing 12/8 with a great bouncy bass line and strings deftly sketching in the passing minor chords like the memory of a sadness that won't quite go away. What makes this one of Madonna's finest choruses is the considerably faster rate of harmonic change: there are parts where it is almost as if there's a chord to every melody note. The bridge has a lovely sliding push rhythm before the harmonica solo adds its sweetness with a subliminal allusion to all those early Stevie Wonder Motown Sixties sides. Just where you expect it to go to a chorus it goes back to the bridge, a clever delaying tactic. There's further invention in the brief 'dub' section where Madonna's backing vocals are supported just by a brass line before the drums kick back in with an exhilarating re-entry.

One of Madonna's strong areas is using countermelodies, and 'Cherish' is a good example of this. By the time we're into the last stretch of choruses there are no less than three melodies going on all at once. Since you only have one voice, if you want to hear this once more you're going to have to play the track again. And again. And again. The single 'Cherish' featured that rarity of rarities, a non-LP track on the B-side, a Madonna/Leonard song called 'Supernatural Thing', for which see the 'Compilations' section.

DEAR JESSIE
(Madonna/Pat Leonard)

THIS WAS released with 'Till Death Us Do Part'. Strings usher in a sentimental but charming children's song, which recalls both The Beatles and Queen in their more playful moods, the former comparison indicated by the trumpet break. In an album that looks back to the traumas of unhappiness in childhood, this song is a celebration of childhood's imagination, a sort of wonderland. As with 'Cherish', vocals are skilfully interwoven on the chorus. The song has the first tempo and time change of a Madonna record, bringing in a child' laughter. It's also sung to herself. If the make-believe land is inside, then it can't be lost. 'Dear Jessie' is a letter to Madonna's own inner child, as well as Pat Leonard's daughter Jessie, who was three at the time. The next section is carried by strummed acoustics. The trumpet break has a slightly Spanish feel, and the glissando evokes the string writing. A song for all young women who keep cuddly toys in their bedrooms. It fades out leaving just the orchestra which is EQ'd to make it sound very thin and trebly as though coming out of a radio. Another theme leads straight into...

OH FATHER
(Madonna/Pat Leonard)

ANOTHER childhood song, this one about her troubled relationship with her father and the child's belief that she was not loved. Madonna uses a contrast of timbre, her higher smoother voice with a lower one. The lyric gets somewhat confused when she brings in the 'Oh father I have sinned'.

A song that would have popularity in the therapy-ridden Eighties, especially with the psychobabble phrase of never feeling so good about herself. There's a very tasteful instrumental break before the vocal bridge where Madonna brings in the realisation that he didn't want to hurt her and why is she running away. One day she can look back and see that he was hurt too. This is probably the most compassionate and generous moment in her music. Some nice echoed slide guitar here.

The track should be compared with the explorations of childhood in the music of Kate Bush and Tori Amos, in particular Bush's 'The Fog' from *The Sensual World* and Amos' 'Winter' from *Little Earthquakes*.

Of the video for this Madonna told the Sunday Times in 1990, "I have resolved my Electra complex. The end of the 'Oh Father' video, where I'm dancing on my mother's grave, is an attempt to embrace and accept my mother's death. I had to deal with the loss of my mother and then I have to deal with the guilt of her being gone and then I had to deal with the loss of my father when he married my step-mother. So I was just one angry, abandoned little girl. I'm still angry. Geffen sent me to a shrink."

KEEP IT TOGETHER
(Madonna/Steve Bray)

To LIFT the mood, an upbeat celebration of the more positive aspects of family life. There's slap bass along with sequenced synth bass. 'Keep It Together' has the individualist breaking out of the family. Here the 'brothers and sisters' cliché of soul music becomes literal. She hits the big time in the city and finds that things are not so good. Your family is gold. The wah-wah synth echoes Sly and the Family Stone and tracks like 'It's A Family Affair'. There's an effective bit of mixing toward the end where the percussion is thinned out. This may well have been cut with a live drummer and conga player. It's a great party singalong track but musically speaking, not particularly inspired.

PRAY FOR SPANISH EYES
(Madonna/Pat Leonard)

Sounds like a bet on a horse. But no, this is a package holiday revisit to the Spanish vibe of 'La Isla Bonita' with castanets but much slower and sombre. The lyric seems to narrate the story of someone going off to fight in a war. Madonna sounds a little edgier than usual on

the chorus, where there's a memorable vocal harmony. It mentions the religious act of lighting a candle. If God exists, does He hear this particular prayer? The impending loss raises the question, why does God allow such things to happen? The melody is quite strong, the second chorus has some trumpet flourishes. The Spanish guitar solo in the middle will appeal to listeners who like Sting's 'Fragile'. The third person quality of this song sits uncomfortably with the other lyrics on the album. There's an effective sudden end with wind chimes left sounding.

ACT OF CONTRITION
('Produced by the Powers That Be')

This is the album's joke ending, which came about when the engineers flipped over the tape of 'Like A Prayer' so Madonna could recite over it. The backing is a reverse version of 'Like a Prayer' with the heavy guitar mixed up loud. Madonna attempts to recite the Catholic act of contrition. It comes to an abrupt end with Madonna repeating 'I reserve. Then I resolve. I have a reservation. What do you mean it's not in the computer!!!'

P.S. Don't bother looking for the satanic messages... whaddya think this is, 'Stairway To Heaven'!? Madonna puts her subversive messages on the right way forward.

Erotica

Maverick WX 491; CD 9362 - 45031-2/ 9362-45154-2;

Released October 1992

ON 20 APRIL 1992 IT WAS ANNOUNCED THAT MADONNA HAD SIGNED A NEW seven-year contract with Warner Brothers. This contract put her at the head of a number of companies of her own under the Maverick label, enabling her to venture into record production, films, publishing and merchandise. Unlike some labels launched by stars which never have any commercial success with anyone else, Maverick has already proved itself in the market place, in particular with successful recordings by the group Candlebox, and Alanis Morrisette. In the preface to her book *The Girlie Show World Tour* (1994), Madonna explained how, "When I finished the *Blonde Ambition* tour, I swore on my life that I would never ever think of going on tour again as long as I lived. I was spent. I was exhausted. I was sick of travelling. I wanted stability. So, I threw myself into making movies, recording a new album, and I also put out a book called Sex. So much for stability."

In October 1992, after a quite a long pause since her last studio album, Madonna released *Erotica*. *Erotica* is in effect a double album. Double albums have an unfortunate reputation for failing to sustain their quality across four sides of vinyl. So often people end up saying that such a record would have made a great single album. Springsteen's *The River* is a good example. *Erotica* is another. Madonna had moved away from the pop sensibility of *Like A Prayer* and the Thirties pastiche of *I'm Breathless* to embrace the recent developments in dance music, notably house, rap and hip-hop. She was determined to move with the times and to ride whatever the main musical current was. It is no accident that a number of the credits to these songs feature samples of other peoples' music. As we have seen, there has always been a tension in Madonna's music between its dance axis and its pop side. The former requires length and has increasingly ditched the distractions of meaningful lyrics and harmonic progression in favour of rhythm. Dance music has become increasingly ascetic in its pursuit of the importance of the rhythm track to the exclusion of other features of music. The requirements of great pop are melody and brevity. A typical dance mix is twice as long as the three minute pop song. Throughout her career Madonna's music has exhibited the conflict of interests caused by her enjoyment of both approaches, and *Erotica* demonstrates this. Where she brings the two into balance, her best music results, and the title track certainly falls into that category. Many of these tracks are too long and could easily benefit from having one to two minutes trimmed off them. Ideas are being killed by repetition.

The reception and assessment of the record were adversely affected by the context in which it was released. *Erotica* was part of the publicity overdrive behind the launch of her limited edition book *Sex*, which featured revealing photographs of Madonna acting out various fantasies (this time sanctioned by herself, in contrast to her early magazine experiences). She held a launch party in Manhattan for the book, where she came dressed as Little Bo Peep with a toy lamb. It should be mentioned that the book came with a CD titled *Erotic*. Demand for *Sex* was such that the initial print run of one million had to be augmented by another 500,000.

This album came from the part of her that voiced the opinion "Art and music can never be too permissive, especially as they're an alternative to the reactionary attitudes of Reagan and the Moral Majority." *Erotica* suffered from being seen as the record of the book. Madonna later said it was a disappointment to her: "I think there's some brilliant songs on it and people didn't give it a chance."

Erotica carries an inscription thanking Shep Pettibone and Andre Betts for bringing out the beast in her. Pettibone said, "All the writing was done at home, in my apartment in Manhattan, and 90 per cent of the production was done there also. It turned out to be a very easy way of working. She'd come over at two in the afternoon, we'd work until eight or nine. She doesn't bring piles of records into the studio. Not at all. In fact, I only did that once – I said, 'Check out this record', but she turned round and said, 'Why would I want to listen to that? I wouldn't want my records to sound like someone else's'". Pettibone also said, "Most of the vocals she recorded for the demos we ended up keeping. The keys for the songs are often lower than she's used in the past. People say it doesn't sound like her but, over the years, she's developed a different vocal quality". He described the album as "pretty dark, introspective, with an R'n'B edge... the songs aren't like 'Cherish', they're talking about something. They are hard and driving and the music is there with it. The techniques I used are like the ones used in the Seventies, we went for the dirty rather than the clean sound everyone goes for nowadays."

Erotica came in two main formats. The 'dirty' version (9362-45031-2) had the track 'Did You Do It?', omitted on the "clean" version (9362-45154-2). It yielded five hit singles, from its release through to the summer of 1993. In August 1993 Madonna then embarked on another world tour, titled *The Girlie Show*, a visual extravaganza, with Madonna sporting a very short blonde hairstyle. This gave her the chance to test some of these songs on a live audience.

EROTICA
(Madonna / Shep Pettibone)

CRACKLE, crackle. What a wheeze! The sleeve states that "all surface noise on the song *Erotica* has been included intentionally". The subtext must be that analogue is sexy and digital is cold, which is ironic when you recall the note on the sleeve of *Like A Virgin* declaring the wonders of digital recording. Madonna wasn't the first to undermine the clarity of the CD medium by adding vinyl crackles, and certainly won't be the last, but it works a treat here. The title track commences with crackle and a low two-note bass riff. The arrangement continues sparse in the vein of 'Justify My Love', but is more upbeat. Listen out for the jumpy funk guitar riff and the swirls of synth strings. Every now and then a dissonant E♯ sounds very high up, a single bell-like note against the F♯ minor key, a technique also used in 'Justify My Love'.

Over all this, Madonna does a spoken dominatrix rap about the pleasures of S&M, complete with a naughty implied rhyme, a word that rhymes with "truck". I'm afraid there were no prizes for this one. The album version of the song is slightly extended, but retains the tight song structure of the single. The chorus features Madonna singing a minor 9th, as in 'Look of Love'. Other nice touches include the use of simultaneous spoken and sung phrases, and the slowed down voice for the phrase "I'm not going to hurt you".

On the coda Madonna gets in some middle eastern scales which also take on a subversive power. 'Erotica' shows brilliant attention to detail throughout, producing a hypnotic groove. Notice the low key ending. The track included a sample from Kool and the Gang's 'Jungle Boogie'. Dance and pop are in balance here.

'Erotica' made the top three on both sides of the Atlantic. It is easily the best track on the album, and one of her best singles. An early version, called 'Erotic', was released on a CD with the *Sex* book.

FEVER
(J. Davenport / E. Cooley)

THIS SONG has been covered many times, most famously as a hit for Peggy Lee in 1958. Madonna's version tethers the melody of the original to a dance drum rhythm, complete with skipping snare drum fills using a beatbox sound which was never intended to sound like acoustic drums. The chord movement of the original is removed. Madonna adds additional words about Pocahontas. There are strings, marimba, and finger-pops at various parts of this track but her voice seems disembodied and detached from the rest of the music. Here the dance ethic which is curiously ascetic in its own way crushes the eroticism out of the song by making everything so regular. One of the main complaints brought against this platter is that Madonna was making supremely unsexy music. A rather sterile track and certainly misplaced as the second track of her first original album in several years. This was also released as the fourth single in March 1993 with plenty of alternate mixes.

BYE BYE BABY
(Madonna/Shep Pettibone)

'FEVER' segues straight into this dance track with a low bass pulsing against a high-pitched Sixties keyboard sound. Madonna's voice is distant and attenuated by equalisation to sound much thinner and trebly, almost as though it were being squeezed through a megaphone. There are occasional flickers of guitar and sampled shouts. Lyrically, Madonna tells a tale of getting rid of a lover. "This is not a love song", she intones and then twists a quote from 'Erotica' – "I'd like to hurt you". It ends with an explosion and her saying "You fucked it up" which is bleeped out. Such a bold gesture of aggression hardly sits well with the erotic vibe and strengthens the air of narcissism and calculation.

DEEPER AND DEEPER
(Madonna/Shep Pettibone/
T. Shimkin)

HERE Madonna is right in the middle of the Nineties disco sound. Stabbing portentous piano, a skipping syncopated drum machine, synth bass, and touches of string above it all. 'Deeper and Deeper' boasts a thicker arrangement than anything else on the album so far. The lyric refers to the influence of mother and father but without the feeling of personal reference that came with the songs on 'Like A Prayer'. The middle eight borrows a chromatic chord sequence on C minor most famously used on John Barry's soundtrack for the James Bond films. This is followed by a Spanish guitar section in G minor with three guitars, one solo, and castanets. In many ways this is the most interesting part of the song. The lyric cobbles together various clichés but really only to prop the tired sexual double entendre of the title. There is also a quote from 'Vogue': "Let your body move to the music".

'Deeper and Deeper' becomes the fourth track to end with just her voice and then move quickly into the next track. It was released as the second single in November 1992, backed by alternate mixes and an instrumental version.

WHERE LIFE BEGINS
(Madonna/A. Betts)

A QUIET beginning leads into a relaxed groove which could be Barry White (without the tonnage). In the background there are long sustained strings with a little funk wah-wah guitar. The drums and bass carry the verse.

Lyrically this is an invitation to oral sex, (and I don't mean talking 'bout love) with Madonna whisking the kitchen/food metaphors for all she's worth to achieve a soufflé of provocation. She even gets in an allusion to Colonel Sanders and his famous chicken! A reasonably strong chorus with staccato on-the-beat chords from the strings. The track even features some slinky piano number It's a little long at 6 minutes but maybe that was deliberate since this album was obviously meant to accompany various nocturnal activities. 'Where Life Begins' manages to be smoochy and driven at the same time, a sort of grade B 'Erotica', expressing the wish that we should all get our just dessert.

BAD GIRL
(Madonna / Shep Pettibone)

THIS STARTS quite slow, with a swing piano and wind-chimes spread across the stereo field, and very quickly establishes itself as having the most interesting chord sequence of anything on the album so far. The verse starts on F# minor and within a few bars has come back to that note, but changed the chord to F# major with an accompanying sense of surprise. Madonna occasionally slips into falsetto to get some of the higher notes. Lyrically, she refers the behaviour of the part of her self that she doesn't like. She's been smoking too many cigarettes and kissing a stranger. Talking to her lover, she explains that she doesn't want to cause him pain but she does and can't help it.

'Bad Girl's chorus is lifted by

the vocal harmony, and is more poppy than any other on the album. Again the track is too long, this time at 5:20. This was released as a single in February 1993 but only just made the top 10 in the UK and stalled at 36 in the US It was backed by a William Orbit mix of 'Erotica', in case you didn't have enough versions already.

WAITING
(Madonna / A. Betts)

ANOTHER song that starts with the sound of scratchy old vinyl before a sliding bass note. The verse is spoken over a sparse accompaniment dominated by a bass line on BF minor that reproduces the tone of Motown bass genius James Jamerson even though it doesn't reproduce anything like the musical interest of his bass lines. After the chorus, a piano chord suggests that we've moved into D minor, but this is an illusion. The rhythm section with a tambourine on the second beat has a very Sixties feel in terms of its sound, and may well be sampled from another record. It may owe something to Marvin Gaye's 'I Heard It Through The Grapevine'. The chorus where Madonna says she's waiting is backed up by spoken voices. The key change is fulfilled on the middle eight that leads to a brief piano solo. 'Waiting' is one of the better tracks on the album. People who like the soul furrow that singer Gabrielle has been ploughing may well enjoy this.

THIEF OF HEARTS
(Madonna/Shep Pettibone)

AH! THE velvet glove that hides the iron fist. Sustained strings are interrupted by smashed glass, Madonna saying 'Bitch'! and audibly chewing gum. 'Thief Of Hearts' takes us back to Nineties disco rhythms. The strings are held for each bar in a thoroughly unimaginative manner. The chorus is pure pop despite the dance scuffling snare drum fills. The lyric is too misogynist, even coming from a woman. The clichés build up steadily. This song is thoroughly melodramatic and dislikeable. The track ends with the broken bottle once more. Police sirens do nothing to help the appeal of the track, and reinforce the general tacky air. For readers of *True Murder Weekly* only.

WORDS
(Madonna/Shep Pettibone)

THE atmospheric G♯ minor chord introduction is ruined by the drum machine's entry which starts another dance track. There is a middle eastern flavour to some of the keyboard parts to this track. A Nation Gasps as Madonna becomes only the 10,000,000th pop singer to use the simile "cuts like a knife". Give me a break. The occurrence of such a cliché in a song that contains a monologue middle eight about communication and advocating authenticity in language is ironic.

Walk it like you talk it. Madonna could help by improving the quality of her lyrics and putting them through a cliché-detector. There's not much of a hook here and not much harmonic return. Here Madonna invokes the proverbial sentiment of actions speak louder than words and links it to her older theme of expressing yourself. The drums are pulled out toward the end to give a respite for a few seconds. It ends with a typewriter. Not so much blue ribbon as black ribbon.

RAIN
(Madonna/Shep Pettibone)

AND TALKING of lyric clichés, ladeez and gennelme... A dark C minor string patch and echoed hi-hat introduce this hit single, which has a stronger chorus and melody, and the tune takes her voice down to the bottom of her range. This lyric plugs straight into the romantic metaphor of love being compared to rain (well, I never) which has been used in countless songs. As everyone knows, in Citadel Pop half the town is in sunshine and the other half in rain. Madonna's invocation of the sun, especially "Here Comes The Sun", puts her in danger of incoherence. There are two spoken voice parts, a key change toward the end from BF major to C major and some nice harmony touches. A pleasant track and more radio friendly than most of *Erotica*. It was the fifth and last single released from *Erotica* in July 1993, with 'Open Your Heart' and

'Up Down Suite' on the B-side. The coda introduces a counter-melody and it winds up with an unaccompanied vocal harmony and the sound of... chips frying. Why does rain on record always sound like chips frying? Or are we back in the kitchen 'Where Love Begins'? We should be told.

WHY IT'S SO HARD
(Madonna/Shep Pettibone)

WELL, SHE'S a fine one to ask...! This returns us to the heavy dance rhythms with a very low bass, piano and sustained strings, with a guitar producing wah-wah sounds. The chorus calls out for unity between brothers and sisters, Madonna being supported by Tony Shimkin, giving the track the feel of something that might be by Seal. The heavy bass line keeps things nailed down. The chords in effect become suspensions over it. There's a nice echoed piano break and the predictable moment where snare and bass are pulled out of the mix while the piano hits off beat chords, and then put back in again. The coda, where Madonna sings "before it's too late" repeatedly is one of the more expressive moments of singing on the record, juxtaposed by a choir of voices. However, 'Why It's So Hard' is over-long.

IN THIS LIFE
(Madonna / Shep Pettibone)

THIS IS a slow track with a three-note keyboard motif that ticks away like a sinister clock juxtaposed against the piano phrases. The lyric is a song of regret for a friend of Madonna's who died of AIDS, a man who acted as a father to her and to whom she didn't have a chance to say goodbye. It is to Madonna's credit that she has campaigned to raise awareness of this issue, to talk about safe sex, and to be prepared to fight AIDS-related discrimination. It's sombre but given the subject-matter avoids the obvious musical approach of going for a big ballad. Lyrically, the chorus is reminiscent of The Beatles "In My Life'.

In the middle eight other instruments take up the three-note keyboard motif. The overall feel is orchestral, almost cinematic, but tends to drag because of the length of the song. The spoken phrases on the coda make the target of the song perfectly clear.

DID YOU DO IT?
(Madonna/A. Betts)

FROM THE sensitive to the boorish. This is a dance track ('Waiting') regurgitated from earlier on the album with Mark Goodman and Dave Murphy rapping over the top of it. Madonna reprises the sung line "waiting for you" from that track. The lyrics are explicit and chauvinistic. It's a tale of seduction in a car. The repetition of the laddish enquiry of "did you do it?" is juvenile. They conclude at the end that he didn't do it. It's astonishing that a woman who implicitly makes so much noise about women standing up for themselves should sully her record with this kind of male chauvinistic piggery. Actually, the back seat of a moving car is not the best place to try and set up your Scalextric. Did you do it? You did? How did you keep the cars on the track?

SECRET GARDEN
(Madonna/A. Betts)

JAMES 'Sleepy Keys' Preston opens this track with some jazzy piano, before another scratchy drum track with a bass line. The verse is spoken. The chorus is sung over a chromatic descending bass line. The lyric plays around with some images of flowers, roses and thorns, lovers, rainbows; almost like a stoned free-association, but without really doing anything with them. This is like a sleepy version of 'Erotica'. What does she still believe?

It lacks interest, there isn't enough going on here. This comes across as an afterthought, generated by musicians noodling around. A low key ending to the album as a whole.

Bedtime Stories

Maverick 936245767-1; CD 9362 45767-2; Released November 1994

THIS ALBUM WAS RECORDED AT NINE DIFFERENT STUDIOS WITH A SMALLER CREW of musicians and some new composers, with whom Madonna was writing for the first time. There are no major stylistic changes to her music; the blend of material remains as before: ballads and up tempo dance tracks. The use of samples, rap passages, drum loops and other arrangement, continued from Erotica insured that her music continued to sound contemporary enough. The title and the sexual theme of a number of the songs are pretty much what you would expect from the follow-up to *Erotica*, although Madonna apparently saw it as more of a love and romance record.

The sleeve note credits Madonna as saying "making this album was a true test of my sanity and stability". Certainly it doesn't sound especially inspired. The dance influence once again cramps her pop sensibility. *Bedtime Stories* works as party music and maybe people use it as a late-night background seduction soundtrack, which may have been intended.

The problem with Madonna's attempts to write sexy music is that she habitually confuses the erotic with the explicit. On a purely musical level, there is nothing sexy about machines and programming. Music made in such a way all too often ends up as synthetic, mechanical, and sterile.

Bedtime Stories comes over as about on a par with *Erotica*, though nothing here can match the power of that album's title track, and it is certainly a long way behind *Like A Prayer*. The title was meant to have a child-like connotation, rather than an erotic connotation. After 1992's book-album blitz on sex, Madonna felt the need to back off and no longer be the Playgirl of the Western World, compulsively seeking out sexual hang-ups in the populace the way Joe McCarthy pursued reds under the bed in the Fifties. Mind you, the fact that the cover showed her with a new Jean Harlow look sprawling across her bed kind of implied that in Metropolis Madonna, it was Business as Usual. Madonna called the record "very romantic". She *told The Face*, "I've been in an incredibly reflective state of mind. I've done a lot of soul-searching and I just felt in a romantic mood when I was writing for it so that's what I wrote about... I decided that I wanted to work with a whole bunch of different producers. Bjork's album was one of my favourite for years – it's brilliantly produced, and I also loved Massive. So obviously, he was on the list. Nellee was the last person I worked with, and it wasn't until then that I got a grip of what the sound of the whole record was, so I had to go back and redo a lot." The lyrics were about romance... or the loss of. Unrequited love."

1994 also saw the publication of *The Girlie Show* (Prion Press), a hardback photo souvenir of Madonna's tour of the same name. Included with it was a live CD featuring the tracks 'Why It's So Hard', 'In This Life' and 'Like A Virgin'.

SURVIVAL
(Madonna/Dallas Austin)

CO-WRITER Dallas Austin has worked with Boyz II Men and a number of R&B acts. Along with 'Human Nature', this song gave Madonna a chance to vent her feelings about the controversies in which she was embroiled in 1992. She commented, "The other songs could be about anybody, but in these two it's quite obvious that I'm addressing the public."

This is a medium-paced dance track which picks up a lyrical allusion from 'Live To Tell'. The vocal is very strong, being double-tracked and harmonised. The rhythm track is powerful but the bass synth line that typified her earlier records is conspicuous by its absence. Clearly, she was anxious to keep up with musical developments in Nineties dance music and 'Survival' does sound Nineties. Her lyrics talk about survival, regardless of the experiences that she goes through. The lyric is full of unsubtle polarised qualities. It deals in opposites: up/down, heaven/ hell, angels/ saints. The disposable quality of the lyric is partly mitigated by the music, which manages to pack the song with multiple hooks.

SECRET
(Madonna/Dallas Austin)

AN ACOUSTIC guitar and little flashes of wah-wah start 'Secret' on a descending chord sequence with Madonna singing over the top. The first chorus is supported by strings. The percussion comes in about the minute mark and when Madonna sings "something's coming over me" the effect of her lower harmony is strangely reminiscent of Nirvana and Kurt Cobain. The lyric talks about a lover who has a secret, and how long it took to understand that happiness lies in her hands. The descending chords on guitar are supported by an ascending string line – an example of contrary motion, a well-known musical device. Each section of the song is strong in itself.

There's a brief wah-wah guitar solo not very high in the mix. Toward the end the melody has an upper harmony to add variety. It's a good track but perhaps, at five minutes, a little long. The drum track is an unvarying loop which adds a touch of monotony the rest of the song just manages to hold at bay for the first four minutes.

Madonna liked this track sufficiently to release a US album of no less than eight different mixes of the track (Sire WPCR 170), and it was the first single from the album.

I'D RATHER BE YOUR LOVER
(Madonna/Dave Hall/Isley Brothers/C. Jasper)

CO-WRITER Dave Hall has also produced Mariah Carey. The backing vocals and bass were supplied by Me'Shell Ndegeocello, another of Madonna's record label Maverick's signings.

The track begins with an introduction in the trip-hop style popularised in the rock field by Portishead on their LP *Dummy*, before turning into swingbeat. A vinyl sample of the drum track adds the grit'n'crackle factor. There's a grinding, smudged five-string bass line keeping busy stirring things up underneath and its the bass which is really the star of this. The hook here is a strange phrase which always arrives in a slightly unexpected fashion. The song is supported by samples from the Isley Brothers and Lou Donaldson. After about three minutes there's a rap where the voice is harmonised for some of the phrases. The last part of the track circles round the chorus and then fades out with Madonna singing "are you surprised?". Me? Nah. But the Isleys might be.

DON'T STOP
(Madonna/Dallas Austin/
Colin Wolfe)

THIS uneventful track stumbles like a sleepwalker on an ice rink through the dance mood, with Madonna delivering a whole string of clichés based on the time-honoured comparison of dancing with having sex. All the right words are here pushing the button like a rivet-puncher on a factory line: groove, doing, moving, grooving, body, get up, rhythm, etc, etc. with a sprinkle of la-de-da picked up from a pawn shop where Annie Hall accidentally left them. The music is forgettable, a sort of rhythm-by-numbers. Madonna doesn't so much stop singing as give up. You may enjoy dancing to this. Or you may yawn a lot.

INSIDE OF ME
(Madonna/Dave Hall/Hooper)

SAME tempo as the previous track but the lyric ambiguity is more interesting. Well, a little. On the one hand, the watery guitar, the sustained strings, the very breathy voices and the naughty bass slides evoke a dripping erotic mood with the photograph of a lover on the mantelpiece. So far, so yum. But on the other hand, the breaths could be of sorrow and the person she has inside of her might be her mother. Hmmmm. People have been awarded the Nobel Prize for figuring out things like this. I guess it's Madonna's "Electra complex" song. There are occasional flurries of dark strings and a sax sample which is repeated at intervals. This is a clear continuation of the approach of 'Erotica'. The moment where the drum track drops out is particularly delicious, leaving just her vocal, possibly the best moment of the whole album - so watch out, y'all. The drums' re-entry would have been much better with a proper fill. You know, one of those human-type skin bashers with the sticks. Keith Moon, where are you when we need you? Not over-long, 'Inside Of Me' is one of the best tracks of the album.

HUMAN NATURE
(Madonna/Dave Hall/
S. McKenzie/K. McKenzie/
M. Deeming)

THIS starts in trip-hop style with heavy bass and drums looping, and Madonna whispering "express yourself, don't repress yourself". Yes, ma'am. I'm ordering my sandbox right this minute.

This is a song of rebellion where the lyric looks back on a relationship in which she was not allowed to speak her mind. Throughout there are whispered phrases which counterpoint the sung lyric. Madonna's voice here copies the Nineties soul style with a very nasal, thin sound which is not very appealing because it sounds so mannered. Michael Jackson, you have a lot to answer for.

Musically the track wears out its welcome by looping around the same four chord sequence for the entire duration. A very bitter, put-down song. The repetition doesn't suggest that the world of the singer is very appealing. Radio stations often censored the song because of the line, "I'm not your bitch / Don't hang your shit on me" when it was released as a single. Madonna says of the track "It's my definitive statement in regards to the incredible payback I've received for having the nerve to talk about the things I did in the past few years with my *Sex* book and my record. It's getting it off my chest. It is defensive, absolutely. But it's also sarcastic, tongue-in-cheek. And I'm not sorry".

FORBIDDEN LOVE
(Babyface/Madonna)

A NOTHER slow track in a mournful minor key with whispered voices. Babyface supplies the male voice on this track, which is a song of desire for that which is forbidden. This is an example of Madonna's pop sensibility getting sunk by the requirements of dance music. Strings come in to brighten up the middle eight, at the end of which Madonna delivers herself of the gem "rejection is the greatest aphrodisiac". The instrumentation is kept sparse so that the vocals essentially carry the track. It fades with Madonna improvising a few phrases over the intro.

LOVE TRIED TO WELCOME ME
(Madonna/Dave Hall)

T HIS opens with a lush string introduction over which a nylon acoustic guitar plays some lead phrases. The verse also carries the occasional silver of wind chimes. The track takes 42 seconds to reach its verse, an unusually long intro. Lyrically, this is a self-confessional song about turning back from love, loneliness and a sense of self-alienation, in which the self is isolated from what she is doing. The winter / hunter imagery is predictable. The mood is subdued, the melody exploring a fairly narrow compass. The second chorus leads to an orchestral break without the drum machine, which is a bit of a relief. Pleasant as the song is, at over five minutes it is too long, and again the monotony of the drum loop with no fills merely exacerbates the effect. Toward the end there are more guitar phrases – a stock-in-trade MOR trademark.

SANCTUARY
(Madonna/Dallas Austin/ Anne Preven/Scott Cutler/ Herbie Hancock)

T HIS IS A bit more ambitious. An atmospheric introduction with assorted odd noises, distant strings, and bits of electric guitar sets 'Sanctuary' as the Dance Cut From One Million Years B.C. Madonna enigmatically declares "Whoever speaks to me in the right voice him will I follow". The ambiguity of the lyric here is caused by the religious overtones of that phrasing. The track settles down into a slow dance groove with an intriguing bass part using minor and major thirds. The electric guitars feature a slowly opening and closing wah-wah pedal. The melody has some interesting intervals.

The religious overtones come out fully in the middle when Madonna intones a Walt Whitman verse from *Motherless Daughters* and adds some moon / water tidal imagery.

'Sanctuary' is the sort of track that draws a frisson of pleasure for the more New Age-minded among her feminist audience. It's probably the most imaginative track on *Bedtime Stories* and I wouldn't be surprised if Steven Speilberg isn't planning on filming it.

BEDTIME STORY
(Hooper/Bjork/Marius DeVries)

A TRACK in which Madonna gets Acid House. This is linked directly with the previous numbers. This is one of Madonna's most artificial ambient dance tracks with a skeletal synth arrangement (over which Madonna groans) and prominent drum machine and machine handclaps. Madonna doesn't have much of a melody to sing and sings it in a subdued manner. The title track is a hymn to the joys of unconsciousness and a rejection of the supposed constraints of reason and language, hence the attack on words with which it starts. This is similar to the sound Everything But The Girl have been being very successful with in recent years. The close of the track has some impressive mixing of the lead synth moving around in the stereo image, so grab your headphones and enjoy. There's an abrupt ending. In contrast to most of the other songs, this is one track that could have been longer and made more trippy than it is. Surprisingly, this was also released as a single in February 1995 in a two-CD set that featured no less than nine mixes.

TAKE A BOW
(Babyface/Madonna)

A NOTHER of the singles released from the album. Typical oriental pentatonics and exotic chop-suey strings produce this ballad with more than just a hint of the Far East. This is Madonna's late-night eastern take-away, written with Babyface who shares the vocals. The verse is sustained through a long descending chord sequence with a few odd twists. It sounds shockingly normal after the ambient 'Bedtime Stories'. The melody is pleasing enough, though sung in the sleepy languid mood which characterises a lot of the vocals on this album. The chorus expresses the theme of saying goodbye to a lover who had taken her for granted. There are clichés aplenty, but at least they're clichés with a toe-hold on the world of music. The title 'Take a bow' should also be credited to a certain D.J. William 'Jellybaby' Shakespeare of hot happening dance city Stratford-upon-Avon, England, who supplied the words about all the world being a stage and everyone having a part to play.

It's over-long at over five minutes and communicates no sense whatsoever of the pain of a real goodbye. It certainly suits the end of an album and will probably have you going out for Chinese spring-rolls or to hire the video of *Enter The Dragon*.

Ray Of Light

Maverick / Warner Bros 9362-46847-2 WE 852 March 1998

AFTER HER PART IN THE FILM *EVITA*, **MADONNA BECAME A MOTHER IN OCTOBER** 1996, giving birth to daughter Lourdes, so named because Madonna hoped she would be a healing influence. During this period between studio albums she became interested in Eastern mysticism and the Kabbalah, and took yoga classes. When she went back into the studio, at Larrabee Studios North, Universal City, California, it was time for a new sound and an opportunity to try a singing voice that had benefited from the coaching she received for Evita. Image-wise it was time for an earth mother goddess look with flowing gold tresses. The Material Girl was about to launch a new phase in her career as the Immaterial Woman.

Ray Of Light was greeted as a come-back and something of a return to form. This album was a UK number 1 and US number 2. In the UK it was her second-biggest selling LP to date. Madonna had always prided herself on keeping tabs on musical fashion. The Prodigy were signed to her label Maverick. French synth-pop band Air had become popular by the mid-Nineties with albums like *Moon Safari*. By hitching up with English dance producer William Orbit she was able to make a record that had enough of an electronic-ambient-dance aura to sound thoroughly contemporary, yet still sound undisputably like Madonna. Orbit had made post-acid house music under name Strange Cargo, and co-wrote six of the tracks, though Madonna made sure the record stayed focused and didn't get too trippy. She called him Billy Bubbles on the sleeve, thanking him 'for sharing my vision and daring to dream'. Most of the album was produced by Madonna and Orbit, though production and writing credits also went to Patrick Leonard and Marius De Vries.

The singles taken from the album feature multiple mixes.

DROWNED WORLD/ SUBSTITUTE FOR LOVE
(Madonna/William Orbit/Rod McKuen/Anita Kerr/David Collins)

FORTY seconds of gentle ambient tones and the stereo oscillations of 'Drowned World' start the album. It rewards listening on headphones to pick out all the small trippy arrangement details and to appreciate the depth of the stereo image (there are sounds close-up and in the background). At 1:31 drums and bass enter and get the song 'Substitute For Love' moving along with its first chorus. This song builds slowly. At 2.00 there are hints of Hendrixy backward guitar in octaves and stereo. Nothing distracts from Madonna's voice. At 2:49 finger-picked acoustic guitar enters, with a few piano notes heavily reverbed in the distance. Electric guitar arpeggios thicken and there's some good heavy drums at 3:45.

Lyrically, the track has Madonna indicating that she is taking stock of her past values: 'I traded fame for love'. It ends with 'This is my religion', signalling the spiritual theme that will run through the record. The vocal is subdued and thoughtful, a tender laying-out of the melody.

She told Q magazine in 1998, 'being popular and loved by people in universal ways is absolutely no substitute for truly being loved. But if you have to have a substitute, it's about the best there is'.

This was one of five singles taken from the album.

SWIM
(Madonna/William Orbit)

THIS STARTS quiet with tremolo guitar on the left and a strummed electric on the right. It will appeal to fans of French pop-synth band Air. Fifty seconds in the big beat enters. Listen for the off-key motif at 1:35, 2:30 and 2:51 – probably Pablo Cook's flute. At 2:45 there is one of those abrupt drop-outs in the arrangement which are typical of Nineties dance music. Echo thickens Madonna's voice and allows her some long-held notes that swirl into the back of the mix. Around the four minute mark there's another finger-picked guitar. On the fade synths approximate waves.

The water imagery continues in this lyric. Madonna told Q, 'there's water in birth and there's water in baptism and when you go into the bath or the ocean there's a feeling of closing, a feeling of starting all over again. Being new, being healed.'

The lyric speaks of the troubles of the world and the ills of society. The sea is seen as the purifying source of life – hence 'swim to the ocean floor'. A song about redemption and renewal.

RAY OF LIGHT
(Madonna/William Orbit/ Clive Muldoon/Dave Curtis/Christine Leach)

ANOTHER OF the singles, 'Ray Of Light' changes the mood to one of joyful extraversion and goes off full charge after an intro with two guitar parts, right and left, whose chords harmonize with each other. The main synth oscillates on the key note as its equalisation (EQ) is slowly filtered between bass and treble. Underneath there's a rock chord riff. Madonna pitches the melody higher than on the first two tracks. At 2:44 there's a synth solo that sounds like it could have come from a Seventies pro-rock record. This may reflect the song's origin as a re-write of a Curtis/Muldoon number called 'Sepehryn' from 1971.

The lyric is upbeat in keeping with the music. Madonna told *NME* (March 1998) was about 'how small I feel in the big picture, but then how life seems to be going by faster than the speed of light and yet if you get outside of yourself and become your own witness you can also stop it.'

CANDY PERFUME GIRL
(Madonna/William Orbit/Susannah Melvain)

THINGS slow up but the thumpy grind of this highly sexual number. 'Candy Perfume Girl' is built on a two-chord F♯-A blues chord change which harks back to the grooves of 'Justify My Love' and 'Erotica'. The rhythm section is mixed very bass heavy and may be a drum sample slowed down because of the 'grit' of the tone. When stuff is slowed down not only pitch changes but frequencies drop and thicken. The

odd synth flourishes across the top of it sound like Obi Wan Kanobe trying to dial a pizza from somewhere out on the edge of the galaxy. After about 2:45 everything drops out except for a mellotron-like keyboard phrase and then return with a resounding bash. The track ends with heavy distorted grunge guitar. At 3:43 and following there are little hints of lead guitar on the left. But R2D2 has the last word...

SKIN
(Madonna/Patrick Leonard)

BIG SYNTH pad chords give 'Skin' a sombre beginning until an oscillating synth drops in pitch. After some intriguing whispers the song gets going with a typical (and rather dull) four-to-the-bar disco dance beat with off-beat hi-hat. There is quite a long echo on her voice and other vocal treatments where a syllable is spun out repeatedly. The verses are in C major but the chorus is in Cm – hence the chill factor on the chorus caused by switching from the major to the minor on the same key note. This is one of the less interesting tracks which underneath the Nineties production comes across as like a Madonna number from the Eighties. The lyric's desperation is off-set by the steam-rollering dance juggernaut, creating an impression of alienation as Madonna's vocal is dwarfed by the bruising beats. At around 5.20 there are hints of Middle Eastern woodwind instruments in the back of the mix. At 6:22 track is probably over-long.

NOTHING REALLY MATTERS
(Madonna/Patrick Leonard)

A NOTHER single, 'Nothing Really Matters' has a delicate ambient beginning as though it is going to be a ballad in D minor. But just before the minute mark the ballad feel gives way to a medium-tempo dance track which recalls Madonna's past – not surprisingly since her long-time co-writer Patrick Leonard had a hand in it. The ambient production touches are restrained, though there is still the odd abrupt bleep across from right to left. There are several faint string lines and parts right in the back of the mix. If you can hear these you get an appreciation of the depth of the stereo field (the front-to-back element). Piano adds a fun solo to the bridge with plenty of off-key notes as it ambles down a couple of bars. Lyrically, this is a song of repentance as Madonna reflects on living selfishly and the law of karma – that everything given comes back to the giver.

SKY FITS HEAVEN
(Madonna/Patrick Leonard)

A DRONE note on D bleeps its way through some typical dance EQ knob-twiddling while echoed electric piano chords fill out the mix. The initial heavy bass and bass drum is

later joined by snare and ride cymbal. The verse creates a strong feeling of gloom not entirely by the chorus. The 'travelling down this road' melody is reminiscent of 'Like A Prayer'. There are a number of atmospheric production touches. Past two minutes listen to the way the chords drift about but the bass note remains the same. After a brief snare drum break the next verse is filled out by an electric guitar part. With references to the 'prophet' and the Gospel this lyric is also reflecting on her spiritual path and following the sun. Listen out for the slowed down drum beat at around 3:50. At the very end a repeat echo guitar phrase gives way to bleeps and a segue straight into the next.

SHANTI/ASHTANGI
(Madonna/William Orbit)

Or Madonna's Passage to India. This is in a long (if intermittent line) of Western songs that attempt to convey something of the 'mystic East' which started with The Beatles' 'Tomorrow Never Knows' and 'Within You, Without You'. The Sanskrit lyric was adapted from a text by Shankra Charya taken from the Yoga Taravali with additional traditional text translated by Vyass Houston and Eddie Stern. Madonna sings over a percussion loop decorated by flickers of electric guitar. Notice this section is harmonically static – it revolves essentially around a single chord. At 1:53 a rock beat is layered over and the Indian tabla drums can be heard on the left. Several times a syllable form the lead vocal is taken, echoed and EQ'd. Toward the end a flute-like instrument takes centre stage. Listen for the sampled three-note melodic phrase 'ah-ah-ah' sung by a massed vocal group. The lyric is clearly religious in the Hindu tradition, a song of worship to the guru who is Self-realized and therefore Enlightened. This would appeal to Kula Shaker fans. The Eastern references of this song set the scene for 'Frozen'.

FROZEN
(Madonna/Patrick Leonard)

THE FIRST single from the album, 'Frozen' is the album's highpoint. It starts with sombre strings in F minor with only over-dubbed percussion and then an 8th note synth pulse. At 52 seconds we get the first exhilirating burst of drum echoed into the distance. This will punctuate the song repeatedly and is sometimes treated with extreme EQ, as after the first chorus when it sounds like an underwater decoration. The chorus has an Eastern-style dance beat. The Eastern influence also comes from the decorated melody doubled on the strings and enhanced in the second chorus when they harmonize the vocal phrase. The bridge has so much of an Eastern feel that at 3:20 we might have strayed into an outtake from Led Zeppelin's 'No Quarter'.

Massive Attack arranger Craig Armstrong deserves much credit for the string arrangement. A simple lyric conceit – that feelings = water and ice = emotional repression is given power and dignity by the focus of the music. The synth touches and strings mean it could almost be a Bond song (if it weren't quite so sombre). One of Madonna's finest tracks, 'Frozen' is a magnificent piece of heavyweight pop. Inspired in part by the film *The Sheltering Sky*, it had a memorable video filmed in the Mojave desert with Madonna looking like a Goth.

THE POWER OF GOODBYE
(Madonna/Rick Nowels)

ENGAGING, classically-styled arpeggios on a four-chord sequence start another of the tracks that made it out as a single. Here Madonna looks back on a love affair that went wrong. The song is one that has a wide appeal with its catchy third and fourth melody phrases in the verse and the nice synth trumpet at end of the first chorus. This is another commercial song which shows continuity with Madonna's earlier output. Again fine strings by Craig Armstrong, especially after the second chorus. Typical of the album are the sustained notes in many of the instrumental parts. The track makes effective use of acoustic guitar to add an 'organic' feel to the second verse and doubled acoustic guitar chords see out the brief coda.

TO HAVE AND NOT TO HOLD
(Madonna/Rick Nowels)

A LEISURELY ambient intro starts this track with its welcome Latin shuffle. Madge's 'ba-ba-ba-ba' scat singing emphasises the Latin beat. In mood this song is very much in keeping with the previous, and shows that the upbeat mood of the early songs fades as the album proceeds. It keeps a steady ambient surface as the minor chords alternate. The music is hypnotically fixed, just as the protagonist of the lyric is fixed on this love that she cannot have – she can only hold. Madonna brings in her little girl lost voice near the end. Perhaps it's not melodically very strong despite the fetching melodic decoration in the verse. Ghostly voices over the strummed acoustic guitars take the song through the slow fade of the coda.

LITTLE STAR
(Madonna/Rick Nowels)

T HIS SONG is about Madonna's daughter. It can perhaps be related to an earlier number like 'Dear Jessie', though it's not as inventive. Clearly having a child and becoming a mother was especially significant to the singer given her feelings about her own mother's early death. This is a difficult lyric subject to tackle without avoiding getting sentimental. This has a lighter touch than many of the album's songs. The high-pitched electric piano

chords lead you at first to expect that Minnie Riperton is about to enter, and the drum-beat remains a rapid rustling rather than a dance thump. Listen out for the unexpected (because out-of-key) G chord toward the end of the verse on the word 'into'. Such moments tend to be in short supply in Madonna's music and were about to become even more so as her music entered the 21st Century.

MER GIRL
(Madonna/William Orbit)

R AY OF LIGHT ends with a brave experiment, probably destined to be skipped by many listeners. This was apparently the first track done and a one-take vocal. Orbit described the studio experience as 'really spooky'. As a synth chord starts like a telephone ringing, Madonna embarks on an autobiographical lyric about her lost mother and her own daughter, about running away from the terrors of life and death. It is unusually descriptive for Madonna and has some powerful lines, such as 'And I smelt her burning flesh/ Her rotting bones/ Her decay'. The basic conceit is that we are all 'fish out of water' - hence the Mer girl of the title. The melody has similarities with that for 'Substitute For Love'. It is as if the intervals have been stretched in time. It makes for a low-key ending to the album.

Music

Maverick / Warner Bros 9362-47865-2 September 2000

HER MUSIC CAREER RESURRECTED BY *RAY OF LIGHT*, MADONNA CAPITALIZED ON the success of her new direction by further exploring an electronica/dance style. To achieve this she asked producer Mirwais Ahmadzai to get involved with the writing and production. A significant figure in French dance music, Mirwais had played guitar in the punk group Taxi Girl which released the *Seppuku* album in 1981, and then worked acoustically with his girlfriend in Juliette et les independants. In 1994 he had gravitated to electronic music and eventually made 'Disco Science' which was a hit on the French club circuit. A friend gave Madonna the record and they hooked up. Mirwais went on to release a solo album *Production* which features another version of one of *Music*'s songs, 'Paradise (Not For Me)'. Nor was William Orbit left out of the picture with a number of credits on the album.

The fundamental elements of *Music* reside in a splicing of electronic effects and beats with acoustic guitar, the whole presented in a 'dry' production sound. 'Dry' here means without the reverb which is used on the majority of records to approximate the sound of music reverberating in a three-dimensional space. For the listener this means that voice and instruments seem to be up close, right on the surface of the speaker. The more ambient qualities of *Ray Of Light* are avoided. The imagery chosen for the packaging dug deep into America's rural iconography, with Madonna lying on straw like a Queen of the Rodeo dressed in cowboy gear. It was a package designed to appeal to the more conservative. What they made of the musical contents is anyone's guess.

MUSIC
(Madonna/Mirwais Ahmadzai)

THE ALBUM'S title track starts with a spoken 'Hey Mr D.J., put a record on' before the vocoder treated voice can be heard. Typical of the production as a whole there's a dry sound with heavy use of EQ to create contrast, as with the treated and echoed voice on the first chorus around the first minute mark. In some ways this is like an updating of the early Eighties Madonna. Prince-like flickers of guitar answering each other left and right. The bridge consists of stabbed keyboard chords. On headphones you can hear the parts and voice wandering around from right to left and back. For all its choppy cut'n'paste technique, 'Music' is harmonically static, being based on a single G minor chord. Whether this is minimalism or a paucity of invention I will leave to you to decide.

Lyrically this is about the uniting power of music. According to Stuart Price, Madonna's musical director for the Drowned World Tour, the rhythmic structure is indebted to Kraftwerk's 'Trans-Europe Express'. This gave Madonna her 12th US and UK number 1s.

IMPRESSIVE INSTANT
(Madonna/Mirwais Ahmadzai)

THIS STARTS with the EQ on higher frequencies turned down so there isn't much treble initially. There are heavily processed vocals and a sample of some kind provides grit and crackle. Some of the sounds have a tactile roughness, making the mix like musical sandpaper. Sudden stops isolate the voice. We get laser noises (always the height of modernity) – like something out of *Star Wars* – and an octave bass line like Seventies disco, but, funnily enough, only one chord, A minor. A manic burbling synth comes in at 2:30. As the track is constructed of various bits there's plenty of sonic repetition. The melody is less than interesting and we have the cliché of ending on the solo vocal phrase. 'Impressive Instant' was used to open her recent live shows. Lyrically, this song talks about being in a trance and lists various cosmic phenomena (including a reference to 'astral bodies drip like wine') but returns to the subject of dance.

RUNAWAY LOVER
(Madonna/William Orbit)

THIS IS taken at a faster tempo with what is known in the trade as a 'driving' dance beat and 'smoking' synth notes above. With all the tenacity of a cat up a greased pole the track refuses to let go of the bass note B, the key note, which is repeated throughout. As is usual with Nineties dance music no parts ever enter or exit musically; they are simply punched in and out with machine-like efficiency. So drums disappear from the mix and enter it again without preparation. Listen for the long example of vocal echo at 2:25 where the signal is allowed to deteriorate as it would if it were an analogue echo. The song ends with vocal repetition which is slowed down so it drops in pitch. The lyric is a rebuke to the 'runaway lover' of the title and includes the witty 'Just like a ship that's lost at sea/You don't care where you drop your anchor/Make sure it doesn't land on me'. Ouch.

I DESERVE IT
(Madonna/Mirwais Ahmadzai)

A SONG FOR Madonna's husband Guy Ritchie is signalled by the sequence of wordplays with 'this guy'. It is an acoustic ballad with double-tracked guitar right and left and uses a three-chord sequence which has served many songwriters, most notably Dylan in 'Knocking

On Heaven's Door'. The 'many miles' section adds another chord to the content. The guitars continue over a tinny drum, while the synths are kept out of the picture until what sounds like a couple of dentist's drills are switched on. The high-point is at 2:50 where a vocal harmony takes the song up a level, an effect that should have been developed further. Overall, 'I Deserve It' is an example of a song where there is not enough interest in the supporting phrases – as much 'Nineties pop. The acoustic guitar playing, for example, is perfunctory and banal.

AMAZING
(Madonna/William Orbit)

Amazing' opens with a pleasing combination of vibes and synths. A string 'pad' enters with the 'voice as Madonna tells a tale of love and desire that she can't get rid of. The production rustles up an arrangement with punch: an attractive rhythm-section Sixties beat topped off with gruff electric guitar arpeggios in stereo. At 2:30 the chorus - 'it's amazing what a boy can do' - is repeated without much instrumentation in the mix before it returns. Madonna even starts to sound a bit like Supremes-era Diana Ross. The coda has some nice piano but it is reached with a crude abruptness. The most engaging track of the album so far.

NOBODY'S PERFECT
(Madonna/Mirwais Ahmadzai)

There are many mysteries in life. One of them is why anyone would want to sully the human voice with a vocoder, and, secondly, why would anyone want to listen to it? But, as Cher has demonstrated, they do. So, welcome to Madonna's own Vocoderville. 'Nobody's Perfect' starts with a whispered vocal intro over a keyboard. The main vocal melody is simply heaven for listeners still waiting for the LP *The Wonderful World of Vocoder*, as the gang let rip with a unit known as an Autotuner. The point about such effects is that they lose whatever appeal they might have had with every repetition. This is used throughout and tends to make Madonna sound less herself and more like a host of other singers as she sings her confession of her own imperfection. Meanwhile, a space-ship flies past the studio and is picked up on the recording at 0:46 and 2:46, and there's a surgically precise Pro-Tooled rhythmic stumble at 1:04, followed by a species of GM feral cat mewling before verse two, before the acoustic guitars rattle under the melting strings. Toward the end of the song another sample from vinyl makes its presence felt with a distinctive needle click.

DON'T TELL ME
*(Madonna/Mirwais Ahmadzai/
Joe Henry)*

ELECTRONICA meets country-rock? 'Don't Tell Me' sounds like the stunted grandchild (skateboard, backward cap) of 'Sweet Home Alabama'. Another single from the album, the intro acoustic guitar of 'Don't Tell Me' has been cleverly edited to sound just like a CD skipping. Of such is progress, folks. The entire song is based on a single four-chord sequence, though some of the mixing disguises this. It has a stuttering beatbox that makes it feel like a ride on a bucking bronco. With a double-tracked lead vocal, Madonna builds some blues phrasing into the melody. The more expressive moments are when strings decorate the sequence toward the end and the intriguing 'loop' just before the fade. This song was based on a composition by Madonna's brother-in-law Joe Henry. It is said that most of the lyric is the same.

WHAT IT FEELS LIKE
FOR A GIRL
(Madonna/Guy Sigsworth)

ANOTHER single, this was written when Madonna was pregnant with her second child Rocco but felt unable to tell anyone. It begins with an extract from the film of Ian McEwen's novel *The Cement Garden* spoken by Charlotte Gainsbourg.

This features a lighter rhythm section, supported by string pads, and a more interesting chord sequence which throws more colour on the melody. Notice the way the drum is pulled out just before the chorus and again later on. Listen for the highly EQ'd bass guitar in the centre. The more ambient production has a more interesting texture of sound floating in and washing around like clouds of tinsel, with a long echo and the vocal pulled back, as Madonna plays with the sensual undertones implied by the title. This is one of the best tracks on the album. The song had a controversial video which was banned by MTV and VH1 and was released as a DVD single.

PARADISE (NOT FOR ME)
(Mirwais Ahmadzai/Madonna)

SOMETHING of a mini-epic, this medium-slow slouchy ballad in A minor gets an arresting start with the juxtaposition of a marimba and a child-like half-whispered voice. There's effective tension between the odd drum rhythm and the distant dark strings. After the first verse a forcefully squidgy synth toothpastes the melody in sliding pitches. The second verse is in French but already the Air influence is obvious. From time to time the vocal is joined by an android. Madonna sounds trampled and sad. 'There is a light above my head', she says at one point before the music plods mournfully on and the strings darken and surge. In some ways a descendant of 'Frozen', this is probably the second best track. Perhaps at 6:33 it's is too long and doesn't have a strong enough ending.

GONE
(Madonna/Damian Le Gassick/ Nik Young)

JUST AS on *Ray Of Light*, the mood in the second half of the record becomes glum. 'Gone' continues the depressed mood of the previous tracks. This has the most 'organic' sound of anything on *Music*. Initially, we have ride cymbal and acoustic guitar with voice. The melody sounds rather unsure, clinging to the root note and the first few notes of the scale, while the drums sound less processed. There is a nice production touch at 1:05 where the guitar clicks into stereo. Madonna then has harmony vocals that momentarily look back to Seventies acts like America and CSN&Y, though neither of those acts would have so disconcertingly collapsed those harmonies onto a single unison note as happens here. With its lyric of sad self-encouragement, 'Gone' is fragile and desperate. It would be interesting to hear this covered by R.E.M.

AMERICAN PIE
(Don McLean)

HERE IS a tale to gladden the heart of every songwriter, as substantial royalty cheques fly to a deserving home. Back in 1972 singer-songwriter Don McLean scored a number 1 with a long but catchy allegory that glanced back to the death of Buddy Holly in Fifties America before giving college students a chance to puzzle out a poetic history of the Sixties. Madonna's cover was featured on the soundtrack of *The Next Big Thing*, along with a song called 'Time Stood Still'. 'American Pie' gives the album the up-beat ending it would otherwise have lacked but doesn't really fit, despite the fact that it compliments Madonna's rootsy image in the cover pictures. Most of the lyric is cut, including anything as specifically historical as Holly's plane-crash, as are the pauses in the original arrangement. Even in this bland form the strength of McLean's song exposes the lack of songwriting craft in most of *Music*.

American Life

Maverick / Warner Bros 9362-48439-2 April 2003

AFTER THE *MUSIC* ALBUM **MADONNA LAUNCHED HER FIFTH TOUR, DUBBED THE** Drowned World tour. She won MTV Europe's Awards for Best Dance and Best Female in November 2000. She married Guy Ritchie in December. Her tour started in Barcelona in June 2001 and would finish in LA in September. Her first tour in eight years, she played guitar on some numbers, both electric and acoustic. The tour was a huge success, the only black spot being the cancellation of a gig at LA's Staples Center on 9/11. In 2001 a second career-spanning compilation appeared, *GHV2*. In 2002 she and Guy starred in a comic film *Swept Away*.

This was her 10th studio album and topped the charts in 14 countries. As usual, the single releases have multiple mixes. The second album produced with Mirwais Ahmadzai pushed the choppy electronic dance/acoustic guitars approach further than *Music* and with diminishing results. The album's downbeat mood is partly caused by the fact that virtually every track is in a minor key.

For the cover, in stark white/red/black, Madonna appeared like a 21st Century Che Guevara with two bleeding gashes on her eyebrow, togged up in military fatigues and toting the wrong kind of hardware. If this was a protest about violence in American life it might just as well have been taken the other way. Unfortunately, events were about to give the album an undesirable context. Pop stars never look sillier than when they're strapped up in bullet belts and come out mouths blazing... only to find that there really is a war going on. As the album was released the tanks rolled into Iraq.

AMERICAN LIFE
(Madonna/Mirwais Ahmadzai)

THE FIRST single off the album starts with Madonna's voice multi-tracked asking whether she'll be a star and sarcastically whether she should lose some weight. The lyric develops as somewhat self-regarding complaint about 'modern life' over a punchy octave synth figure synchronized with the bass drum beat. The song stutters with violent transitions. Acoustic guitar adds a touch of pathos, representing a lost innocence, until you hear the fact that it's a sample being repeated. After three minutes there's a Madonna rap which lists all the people who work for her. She's just living out the American Dream but it isn't what it seems.

The dry production sound is typical of the album. She told Q, 'I've had twenty years of fame and fortune, and I feel that I have the right to an opinion on what it is and what it isn't.' There's a 'clean' version of the album which presumably omits the four-letter word that features toward the end of the track.

HOLLYWOOD
(Madonna/Mirwais Ahmadzai)

THIS WAS the second single and is arguably more interesting that the title track. It certainly flows better. On the intro birdsong is heard before acoustic guitar sets off a four chord sequence which reminds me of the Red Hot Chili Peppers. Then drums and synth take over. At the one minute everything is pulled out leaving the voice and acoustic guitar. It has a sinister lyric theme but doesn't take it far enough – just the usual stuff about Hollywood as the place of stars and illusory dreams. 'How could it hurt you when it looks so good?' she asks. There's an abrupt shift of key at about three minutes from B minor to C# minor, such tone shifts being the commonest key changes in pop, utilised to give a song's closing choruses extra sparkle. There's another rap on the phrase 'push the button' during which her voice is slowly morphed lower in pitch.

I'M SO STUPID
(Madonna/Mirwais Ahmadzai)

A TWO-CHORD electric guitar idea provides the initial platform for this song. Then drums come in with a minimal beat. The lyric expresses disillusionment: 'I used to live in a fuzzy dream' sings Madonna, and she concludes that her younger self was 'stupider than stupid'. The guitar shifts to the left as the song tries a three-chord minor change. The chord sequence leans heavily to the minor, which gives it a sombre feel. At 2:15 a synth drifts up and down on the octave and is treated with fx but doesn't open up into anything. This is probably the best song on the album so far – but lacks interesting melodic parts in the arrangement. 'Everybody's looking for something... Everybody's stupid, stupid' is the song's pay-off line. Toward the end there are guitars right and left so the electronica takes a back seat.

LOVE PROFUSION
(Madonna/Mirwais Ahmadzai)

TRACK four starts with another acoustic guitar start on the four-chord. Bm F#m A E sequence. There's jiggery-pokery with her vocal at certain points. 'I got you under my skin' is the repeated lyric line. Rhythm is supplied by a crude four-to-the-bar bass-drum which drops out or returns abruptly. On the chorus her voice is supported by a male backing vocal holding sustained 'ahs'. At the

2:30 mark there are some atmospheric synth string parts buried at the back of the mix. The main synth figure which is supposed to add interest is uninspired. It ends with the cliché of the voice that is suddenly left on its own for the words 'feel good'.

NOBODY KNOWS ME
(Madonna/Mirwais Ahmadzai)

THIS features vocoder-treated vocal over a bleeping synth, again on a minor chord. Heavy drum hits stress the melody during the verse. With its dull melody this must surely be one of the most forgettable songs she has ever recorded. 'Nobody knows me', she sings repeatedly, along with references to social disease, which could be a metapho ... At least it's good to hear her saying she doesn't watch TV.

NOTHING FAILS
(Madonna/Mirwais Ahmadzai)

ONCE more, acoustic guitar leads off over light drums and a single low-pitched vocal. This is a love song based on a simple four-chord sequence in B♭. Lyrically it talks about a lover who is the one and how their meeting was not chance. There's a hint of cello early on, and reference to her having climbed the Tree of Life. 'I'm not religious' but she wants to pray. This is the key line of the lyric, time for a gospel choir to provide fast-food spiritual suste-

nance. M's vocal is multitracked during this section. At 3:45 we go back to guitar, rhythm section, one synth, then the vocal. The strings add some interest.

INTERVENTION
(Madonna/Mirwais Ahmadzai)

BY THIS point in the album it is hard not to feel a distinct sense of repetition. Yet again a track starts with a simple three chord minor sequence over which Madonna sings. Then an acoustic guitar comes in on the right, and then a second on the left (detuned by a tone to make it sound deeper). The chorus has a four-chord turnaround. The arrangement is light in terms of the low number of parts, virtually minimal until the final choruses. There are the usual abrupt endings to the parts to emphasise the cut-ups. Lyrically, the song is optimistic about how the relationship will last, with references to 'the road looks lonely but that's just Satan's game'. Listen for the section around 3:15 where Madonna sings the chorus words over the verse chords. Bass synths come in toward the end to beef it up.

X-STATIC PROCESS
(Madonna/Mirwais Ahmadzai)

GUESS what? Another song that starts with acoustic guitar and voice. In this instance it's the same three chords as the previous track except in A minor offered up with a bit of ham-fisted finger-picking. Again too many of the songs sound samey. 'Jesus Christ will you look at me/don't know who I'm supposed to be?' on the bridge. There are several vocal lines, with moments of two-part harmony, and points where different words are sung simultaneously. At two minutes an organ-like sound comes in but again plays nothing of melodic interest. It's an ambivalent lyric: he's beautiful and talented but she forgot she was special also and just as good as him; good to get that clear.

MOTHER AND FATHER
(Madonna/Mirwais Ahmadzai)

A TINNY Eighties sounding three chord sequence gets this going. Then a bass drum beat comes in and flickers of Eighties disco guitar. The oddly timed rhythmic stabs in verse two add some interest. Singing in her higher register, the lyric refers back to childhood experience – her absent mother in particular, with a recognition of the need to let past suffering go, and her rejection of her father. She analyzes her predicament in terms of being a victim of a rage from childhood. She told Q it was 'a way of letting go of the sadness and moving on'. This is the kind of track that has people wittering on about this album being 'introspective' and 'serious'. But when the lyric can only rise to the level of lines like 'There was a time I had a mother – it was nice' such claims are risible. Madonna has yet to make an album that profoundly engages with her past, that is artistically satisfying and articulate, in the way that artists such as Dylan or Kate Bush have managed.

DIE ANOTHER DAY
(Madonna/Mirwais Ahmadzai)

T HE THEME song to the MGM James Bond film starts with an exciting flourish of bows on strings, and for the first eleven seconds it seems as though we might be in for a treat. However, the song is never allowed to breathe because of the stuttering editing – as if someone hasn't pushed a lead in properly somewhere - which keeps cutting out the signal. It reveals much about the decline in songwriting quality since the early Bond songs. Melodically uninteresting and harmonically repetitious, the sole enjoyment lies in the strings, especially the chord at 2:20. Otherwise, it's a matter of more flatulent synths. Elton John famously described this as 'the worst Bond tune of all time'. It certainly isn't a patch on the song Garbage did for *The World Is Not Enough*. Mind you, the 'Sigmund Freud analyse this' is the wittiest line on the album.

Madonna's 'Blonde Ambition' hairpiece was dropped after the initial US dates as it was damaging her real hair.

Madonna steals the show with her
Marilyn Monroe tribute at the 1991
Oscars ceremony.

Erotica (1992)

A harsh new look for the 'Girlie Show' in 1993.

Madonna performing 'Bedtime Stories'
at the Brit Awards in London, 1995.

A *Bedtime Stories* outtake.

Performing 'You Must Love Me' from *Evita* at the 1997 Oscars.

At the MTV Music Video awards, Los Angeles, September, 1998. at which Madonna won Video Of The Year for 'Ray Of Light'.

Ray Of Light (1998)

At the Grammy Awards, 1999, performing, 'Nothing Really Matters'.

Cowboy chic at the European MTV Awards, 2000.

Music (2000)

Performing 'Candy Perfume Girl' on the opening night
of her 'Drowned World' tour.

On stage in Paris during the 'Drowned World' tour, June, 2001.

Madonna playing guitar on stage for the first time during 'Drowned World'.

American Life (2003)

On stage in Barcelona at the opening
night of her 2003 world tour, June 9.

EASY RIDE
(Madonna/Mirwais Ahmadzai)

S TRINGS play the solo intro – easily the most musical passage in the song before strummed acoustic guitar leads into another minor key ballad and the strings return to tart up the second verse. Madonna albums often end with downbeat songs and this is no exception. It is saturated by the unhappiness which dominates much of her music. From 3:20 we get choppy strings with a solo voice – another good bit which doesn't last long. After four minutes there's a loud synth dead centre and snatches of electric guitar. The strings are now chopped up but allowed to play a bar or two to finish. The album ends with Madonna singing about going round in circles.

FILM SOUNDTRACKS

Vision Quest / Crazy For You

Geffen GEF 70263; Released 1985

THIS IS THE FIRST OF THE SOUNDTRACK ALBUMS WHICH CLUTTER MADONNA'S discography. Here, she contributed a couple of songs to *Vision Quest*, a film directed by Harold Becker and produced by Jon Peters, and starring Matthew Modine as a young man determined to achieve sporting success but who loses his lover along the way. This not very successful film gave Madonna a small part as a nightclub singer, performing three songs. In the UK the film was re-titled *Crazy For You* to cash in on her success when it was issued on video. These two tracks both came out as singles by Madonna, with songs by other artists on the B-sides. 'Crazy For You' was deemed worthy enough to be included on the *Immaculate Collection* greatest hits of 1989. These are the only Madonna songs on the soundtrack album.

CRAZY FOR YOU
(John Bettis/Jon Lind)

THIS SONG was produced by 'Jellybean' Benitez and mixed by Shep Pettibone and Michael Hutchinson. Compared to Madonna's previous hit singles, 'Crazy For You' exhibits a slight increase in sophistication. The intro to the song features a woodwind melody and an electric guitar chord sliding from one position to the next, motifs that occur several times through the song. The spacey quality of most of the verse is due to the snare drum only coming on the last beat of the bar. The fuller rhythm doesn't start until just before the chorus. Otherwise, the verse is carried by a harp sound, some bass synth and a chattering single note guitar line. The melody has some interesting turns in it, allowing Madonna to push her voice a little on the higher parts. There is a boldness about the chorus which certainly suits a film song. There is less repetition of the chord sequence than on her other early singles, and the chorus in particular does not revolve around a sequence but slowly unravels to its climax. This went to number 2 in the UK with Sammy Hagar's 'I'll Fall In Love Again' on the B-side.

GAMBLER
(Madonna)

PRODUCED by 'Jellybean' Benitez and arranged by Steve Bray, this is an upbeat synth-disco number in the style of Madonna's first LP, though it is perhaps less repetitive than most of the songs on that album. It starts with drums, electronic handclaps, and percussion, which is soon joined by a bass synth line and then higher stabbing keyboards. The song moves quickly through an initial four-chord chorus and a brief three-chord verse, eventually reaching a middle eight where Madonna sings some heavily echoed low phrases. This section sounds a little like Blondie and returns a little later in the song. The lyrics are typical - Madonna asserting her independence and daredevil attitude to life to a lover who obviously just won't be able to stand the pace. The coda uses a new musical sequence with an echoed "You can't stop me now" and some whistling. The rapid movement through the various sections can't save the song from being fairly ordinary but it passes quick enough. Bit like 24-hour flu, really. The single was backed by Black N'Blue's 'Nature Of The Beach' and went to number 4 in the UK.

Who's That Girl

Sire UK WX 102; CD 925611-2; released August 1987

FOLLOWING HOT ON THE HEELS OF HER SUCCESS IN *DESPERATELY SEEKING SUSAN*, *Who's That Girl* was another stab at cinema success. Madonna played the character of Nikki Finn, a young woman accused of homicide who insists that she is innocent. Released on parole, she is determined to clear her name. Along with a character called Loudon Trott, who is supposed to get her on a bus back to Philadelphia, she gets caught up in 36 hours of high adventure, culminating in a scene where Nikki interrupts a wedding to announce the identity of the real murderer. Madonna said of the film's heroine, "I had a lot in common with Nikki. She's courageous and sweet and funny and misjudged. But she clears her name in the end, and that's always good to do. I'm continuously doing that with the public. I liked Nikki's tough side and her sweet side. The toughness is only a mask for the vulnerability she feels."

The soundtrack album includes four songs by Madonna, the other artists being Club Nouveau, Michael Davidson, Duncan Faure and Scritti Politti. But the sequencing put three of hers first, and with her face on the cover, *Who's That Girl* became a sort of Madonna album by default. With the exception of 'Can't Stop', Madonna's songs were all hit singles. The film was to be called *Slammer* but Madonna allegedly couldn't come up with something that fitted that title and when the title song's lyrics were written a change of title for the film seemed appropriate. Madonna said of the film's music, "I had some very specific ideas in mind, music that would stand on its own as well as support and enhance what was happening on the screen and the only way to make that a reality was to have a hand in writing the tunes myself ... (the) songs aren't necessarily about Nikki, or written to be sung by someone like her, but there's a spirit to this music that captures both what the film and the character are about, I think."

Who's That Girl went some way to fill the gap between her own album releases. 1987 was the year of a long concert tour that saw her playing to enormous crowds in the US, Europe and Japan. Video highlights were issued as the *Ciao Italia* video. In the end the film was a flop but the title track gave her a number 1 and 'Causing A Commotion' was a number 2.

WHO'S THAT GIRL
(Madonna/Pat Leonard)

DELIGHTFUL. Pat Leonard has described the genesis of the track: "Madonna called up saying that she needed an up tempo song and a down tempo song. She came over on a Thursday and I had the chorus. She went in the back room with a cassette of that. I worked out the rest of the parts, she finished the melody, she went back in the back room (and) she finished the rest of the lyrics.

"She came out and said, 'We'll call it "Who's That Girl", and I think it's a better title for the movie than *Slammer* so we'll change the name of the movie, too.' She sang it once and that was it. We put guitars on it and percussion the next day."

This is one of Madonna's best takes on her original musical style. All the usual ingredients are here –

the drum machine, the bubbling bass synth line, the distant string sound – yet 'Who's That Girl' is the first Madonna song of which the chorus could be described as having a haunting quality. All three parts of the song are as strong as each other – the verse, the chorus and the bridge (used twice) where Madonna sings "what can help me now". Along the way a slight Hispanic flavour is added to the proceedings by the Spanish phrases sung on the chorus, by the trumpets on verse 2 and the instrumental break... Above all, it's another of those songs by Madonna (like 'Cherish') where multiple vocal lines make a wonderful chorus. This is an effect that goes way back to the roots of pop in group vocal singing. A song like the Beach Boys' 'God Only Knows' or 'I Get Around' combines several lead lines on its fade-out, a trick revived to brilliant effect on R.E.M.'s 'Near Wild Heaven' and 'Fall

On Me'. On the last choruses of 'Who's That Girl' there are three or four different vocal hooks all entwined. Magic.

CAUSING A COMMOTION
(Madonna/Steve Bray)

A NOTHER track very much in Madonna's dance up tempo groove with an arrangement made up of a host of parts all contributing a bit here and a bit there. The track wastes no time getting down to business by starting with a chorus. The verse is carried by a four-note descending bass line and staccato chords punching in. The lyric knowingly makes a reference to getting into the groove and there are about three parts to the vocal harmonies. Perfectly acceptable, though not in the same class as 'Who's That Girl'.

THE LOOK OF LOVE
(Madonna/Pat Leonard)

T HIS IS in no way related to the Burt Bacharach/Hal David tune covered so huskily by Dusty Springfield, but was in fact a song written the day after 'Who's That Girl'. 'The Look Of Love' is the album's other gem, starting with a low bass synth line and an atmospheric backing that gives a sense of space; light percussion, and a high register note that contrasts with the deep bass. The last verse has an attractive acoustic guitar figure and the last chorus thickens up the sound by

adding a chorused guitar part. One especially expressive moment comes each time Madonna sings the word "look" over the D minor chord underneath. She sings this word on the second note of the scale, creating the distinctive stabbing poignancy of the chord known as a minor ninth. This is also featured on the hook of 'Erotica'. There is also a two-part vocal on the line "no place to run" which adds to the overall interest. An expressive, understated track.

CAN'T STOP
(Madonna / Steve Bray)

M EANWHILE, back on the dance floor, this is a bright, breezy song with stabbed chords all round and a thoroughly squiffy keyboard that sounds like it has gone AWOL from a Prince record. This fits neatly into sub-genre number 374 in the catalogue of Pop Lyric Subjects: I want my man and I'm going to get him whatever. There is a slight feeling of Sixties motown: at a pinch it could just be a Four Tops or Martha Reeves and The Vandellas track. The instrumental break is really a chorus with a synth line over the top. The track is rather too long, at 4:45. 'Can't Stop' is a good example of the tension in Madonna's music between the requirements of dance music, where length is important – why stop a good groove when you're getting down? – and the requirement of classic pop, which is say what you gotta say in 3:30 and then out.

I'm Breathless -
Music Inspired By The
Film *Dick Tracy*

Sire WX 351; CD 925209-2; released May 1990

THIS SOUNDTRACK ALBUM WAS A MAJOR MUSICAL DEPARTURE FOR MADONNA.
The film, starring Warren Beatty, was an attempt to recreate the world of cartoon detective Dick Tracy, from the strip by Chester Gould first published in October 1931, set in the seedy underworld gangster-ridden of the Thirties. Beatty had acquired rights to the film in 1985 and it was finally Disney Pictures that gave him a budget of 25 million to make it, hoping for a popular success that would rival *Batman*. Madonna told *Premiere* magazine that "Everybody said I would be perfect for the film... I waited and waited for Warren to call me. He never did. Finally, I decided to be pushy and called him. It took him a year to make up his mind." Madonna's part involved playing the role of Breathless Mahoney, a part written for her, since Mahoney was not one of the original strip characters. Hence the joke implied in the title – "Who are you?" "I'm Breathless." "Why, did you run up some stairs?"

She was to be a vamp, with plucked eyebrows, low-cut dresses and blonde hair, and Beatty decided that she should sing three songs by Stephen Sondheim. Madonna admitted to finding them difficult at first. Off screen the tabloids had a field day sighting Beatty and his leading lady enjoying their much-publicised affair. In the end, Madonna's lust for fame got too much for him to handle, as a famous scene in the *Truth Or Dare* film shows. Filming began in February 1989 and the film was released to a media blitz on June 1990. Madonna later said, "I was nervous about it but I've had a lot of positive opinion about it. It's definitely the best movie I've been in, and Warren Beatty was the best director I've worked with." Shot in primary colours with some actors wearing grotesque face-masks, the film had small roles for Dustin Hoffman and Al Pacino, and received several Oscar nominations.

Dick Tracy yielded no less than three separate soundtrack albums. A singer/songwriter called Andy Paley composed a number of songs in a Thirties style which were then recorded by many famous singers; composer Danny Elfman created an album's worth of instrumental and orchestral music; and finally Madonna produced an album of her own, *I'm Breathless*, which included the three songs from the film – 'Sooner Or Later', 'More' and 'What Can You Lose' – written by Stephen Sondheim.

The soundtrack needed to duplicate the music of the period. To this effect, Stephen Sondheim supplied three jazz influenced songs, and Paley two more. Since the harmony and melodic lines of that style are more complex than pop music and less dependent on rhythm, this was to present Madonna with the most demanding singing of her career to date. She talked of the 'chromatic wilderness' of the tunes, and admitted, "I wasn't sure I could do them justice and neither was he. But Stephen gave me a lot of encouragement. It was a great learning experience for me. I remember when I first heard the music I panicked. I thought I can't sing these, they're too difficult." To the surprise of many, she coped reasonably well. Who would have thought that the shrill voice of tracks like 'Holiday' would have been capable within five years of handling this material. But so it was.

Despite Madonna's laudable efforts in the vocals department, the whole album fails to transcend the sterile, preserved-in-amber quality of pastiche. It does have one of Madonna's most successful dance tracks, 'Vogue', and several entertaining songs like her duet with Beatty, 'Now I'm Following You', which is a genuinely funny musical joke. The album was recorded in three weeks, and in 1994 she told *Q* magazine, "I would have to say that the favourite record I've made is the soundtrack to *Dick Tracy*. I love every one of those songs."

HE'S A MAN
(Madonna/Pat Leonard)

THE ALBUM kicks off with a blast of voice over an intercom and a slow, threatening shuffle, with a descending chromatic melody that is the stock-in-trade of detective films the world over. The melody has some tricky intervals and turns in it which Madonna negotiates well. This is the character 'Breathless' singing to Dick Tracy. The chorus line is "You're a man with a gun in your hand".

Her voice is a little light for this song. It really needs someone with a more powerful voice – say Tina Turner or Shirley Bassey – though she does try to deepen her tone. It's unusual to hear Madonna's voice in the middle of a relatively denser arrangement with organ, strings, piano, sax and backing vocals. The voices return for a section in the middle. 'He's A Man' is a reasonable opening track for a soundtrack album. There is a key change to lift the track toward the end. It never quite sends the shiver down the spine that, say, a John Barry number like 'Goldfinger' or 'Thunderball' does.

SOONER OR LATER
(Stephen Sondheim)

THIS IS a typical Thirties jazz smoochy ballad with comping piano, brushes on the drums, double bass and horns. It conjures the atmosphere of a smoky nightclub at two in the morning, the last few couples still swaying arm in arm around the dancefloor. It has a nice live feel. The melody is especially sinuous, moving through a variety of unpredictable shifts and turns. Sometimes the melody takes Madonna perilously close to the bottom of her range. As with the opening track it would suit a stronger voice. 'Sooner Or Later' was nominated for an Academy Award in 1991 and Madonna performed it at the ceremony.

HANKY PANKY
(Madonna/Pat Leonard)

A SONG in which Madonna waxes lyrical about handkerchiefs. Or perhaps not. This grew out of a line in the film where Breathless says to Dick Tracy, "You don't know whether to hit me or kiss me" – a sentiment which may also express how part of the world feels about Madonna. The track has a false intro with piano and strings, quite slow, before it suddenly springs into life into a jazz-boogie with a walking bass line and a shift from minor to major for the chorus. The lyric has Madonna extolling the virtues of a good spanking and features the important line, "my bottom hurts just thinking about it" which reoccurs in the duet with Warren Beatty.

Asked by American chat show host Arsenio Hall whether the song expressed her own feelings on discipline (ahem) Madonna replied, "I don't like it really hard, though. Just a little stinging and it's good." It was to prove controversial, despite its inane nature, which only goes to show that if Madonna didn't exist, it would certainly be necessary to invent her.

This may just be the coldest so-called erotic record ever made. Come back Jane Birkin and Serge, all is forgiven. It's my nominee for the annual My-Ding-A-Ling-Oh-Shucks-But-You-Shouldn't-Have Award for a terminally inane single. *Sky* magazine called it "possibly the worst single in the history of the universe". Madonna apparently had to tone the lyrics down a little to please the Disney censors who were worried about their family image. It went to number 10 in the US and number two in Britain.

A while after, Madonna explained, "It's a joke. It started because I believed that my character in *Dick Tracy* liked to get smacked around... I despise being spanked. I was just playing with Arsenio... I certainly punish myself in lots of ways but not by having people hit me... I thought it would be obvious – because of my image as a person who wants to be domineering and take charge – that there was no way I would actually want someone to spank me."

I'M GOING BANANAS
(Michael Kernan/Andy Paley)

FROM one inane song to another. This is a hymn to investing in fruit and vegetable shares. It's a medium tempo song in Latin American salsa rhythm in which Madonna sings in a strange, squeezed vocal, a lyric comprising bits of dog Spanish. Peel back the arrangement and marvel at the backing's mouthwatering curve of shouts, percussion, and blasts of brass. This is one brief fruit cocktail of a song. Party music for when everyone is feeling very silly. (And I lied about the shares.)

CRY BABY
(Madonna/Pat Leonard)

ANOTHER shift of voice by Madonna, this time to a gum-chewing gangsters-moll, the sort who would pronounce "bird" as "boyd". The melody is strong and comic over a backing of synth strings, horns and trumpets, and a rocking bass. The horns provide a counter-melody. Muted trumpets squeak and wail in the background. The lyric is about a guy who is too sensitive and much too soft. "Knock it off", says Madonna over some fake theatrical sobbing. The bridge is a sickly chromatic chord sequence which slips and slides, echoing its subject's lack of spine. There's a long fade when a sudden ending would have been more in keeping. One of the better pastiches on the record.

SOMETHING TO REMEMBER
(Madonna/Pat Leonard)

A SONG that later gave its title to the 1995 collection of her ballads. This is a slow slinky number with restrained but slightly funky electric piano supported by strings and delicate percussion. The chord sequence has many unexpected shifts and the melody is equally unpredictable in the way it changes direction. The music's unpredictable jazz changes have the effect of bracing the tune against sentimentality. The emotion here is a little more complex than in Madonna's chart hits. Lyrically, the words sum up a love affair which hasn't worked out but out which some good has come. The message of the song, from the departed lover, is "love yourself". The last part of the song has drums to kick it along. The coda is a solo piano passage.

BACK IN BUSINESS
(Madonna / Pat Leonard)

ANOTHER slow, smooth song with a rising motif and finger-clicks for the verse. There is a sax line, and sampled vocal do-do's are triggered in the background. The chorus bursts into life, with Madonna clearly relishing the lyrics about good guys finishing last, and putting in the spoken line about not knowing whether to hit her or kiss her. The coldness of her delivery is apt for the topic. There are some pleasingly creepy chords changes and the song as a whole has a very strong dynamic contrast between the sparse atmospheric verse and the driving chorus.

Toward the end there are some cutesy backing vocals with Madonna adding a bit of scat-singing and imitating a muted trumpet. A sax solo brings this song to an end, one of the more interesting cuts on the album.

MORE
(Stephen Sondheim)

THE B-SIDE of the 'Vogue' single. Sprightly piano chords drive this almost Charleston-sounding medium tempo song complete with typical syncopated push chords, changes of tempo, and wonderfully contrived rhymes like rhythm / with 'em.' Once the drums enter the song turns into a real Broadway number set up for swanning around a stage in sequins with male dancers, in a roving spotlight. There's even a tap-dancing break which demonstrates how well it would translate straight on to the stage. Lyrically, Madonna sings a tale of how even with riches, she just wants more and more. There are lots of stops and starts in the arrangement and the lyric brings the words at breakneck speed which requires careful enunciation. For the last few verses there's a key change up a semi-tone. The ending is thoroughly kitsch, with lines being echoed by the girl chorus and a long passage in

free time before everyone comes in for the big finish. Bring down that curtain!

WHAT CAN YOU LOSE
(Stephen Sondheim)

THE VOCAL on this is shared with Mandy Patinkin, who sings the first verse over the solo piano number Patinkin won a Tony award for the part of Che in the Broadway production of *Evita* and was Sondheim's choice for his Pulitzer prize-winning musical *Sunday In The Park With George*.

Madonna's higher voice enters on the second verse with the strings, then the two voices start harmonising. A short and schmaltzy ballad.

NOW I'M FOLLOWING YOU (PARTS 1 & 2)
(Andy Paley/Jeff Lass/ Ned Clafin/Jonathan Puley)

THESE tracks are probably the most entertaining on the album. Part One is a Twenties tune where Madonna shares the vocal with Warren Beatty over strings and horns and muted brass. There's another tap-dancing break over the piano solo and a slight blues influence on the turnaround. The trickery starts when the record gets stuck on the last chord. You then hear a needle being dragged across the vinyl. This leads to a highly EQ'd repetition of Part One as Part Two, made trebly with a hilarious Eighties dance drums and bass synth superimposed. This creates the bizarre imposition of Madonna and Breathless Mahoney. The darker themes of 'He's A Man' return complete with a variety of special effects including the intercom voices. A number of fragments start to get pasted over various sections. At one point, several of Beatty's sung lines are slowed and speeded-up. Madonna gets in her joke - "Dick – that's an interesting name". Her pronunciation of Dick' is then sampled and used to play the main melody with comic results. The main tune comes back and then the song ends abruptly with Breathless taking the record off her 78 player, once again scratching the record. A rollercoaster.

VOGUE
(Madonna/Shep Pettibone)

THIS SONG had nothing originally to do with the film, but the lyric's citation of a number of famous Hollywood actresses, including Marilyn Monroe, Dietrich, Grace Kelly, Ginger Rogers, Rita Heyworth, Kathleen Turner, Greta Garbo, Jean Harlow and Bette Davis, gave it a suitable connection. 'Vogue' came out of a collaboration with Pettibone when they were allegedly trying to compose some B-sides. Pettibone said the intention was just to make a fun dance record. The song's title alludes not so much to the magazine of that name but to an activity indulged in some of New

York's transvestite dance clubs, where people would dress up and act out the gestures and stereotypical poses of models as seen on the cover of a magazine like Vogue.

Madonna felt that the song might not be strong enough to be an A-side but others at the record company persuaded her to change her mind. This single was her eighth number 1 record in the US, and her seventh number 1 in the UK thus making her the most successful solo female singer in the charts.

'Vogue' returns us very strongly to the Nineties. Its exuberance feels as though Madonna has, with relief, dropped Breathless and the ornate harmonic progressions of jazz. With the cry "strike a pose" repeated, the track gets underway with a dance rhythm clearly related to 'Justify My Love' in parts, but also sounding very like the UK's Human League. High strings persist throughout, and there's a punchy syncopated piano on the chorus. The message of the lyric is Madonna returning to the vitality of dancing as an act of individual imagination and expression – let your body go with the flow. For the middle eight Madonna begins her rap of famous actors and actresses on the cover of a magazine – ladies with an attitude. Beatbox drum sound and the snare rolls as usual. 'Vogue' is one of Madonna's more effective dance records. The track ends with an echo of the title. It's surprisingly short considering it's for dancing – but is all the stronger for that.

Evita: Music From The Motion Picture

Warner Bros CD We 893; released November 1996

MADONNA'S NEXT VENTURE INTO FILM AND ONE OF HER MOST AMBITIOUS roles to date was to play the part of Eva Peron in Alan Parker's film version of the successful Andrew Lloyd Webber/Tim Rice musical *Evita*. The musical was first staged in the mid-Seventies and the London cast recorded a version in 1978, which has a number of other tunes not included in this recording. Filming took place through most of 1995. It has been said that Meryl Streep was at one time going to take the role of Eva Peron and also that Andrew Lloyd Weber thought Madonna too old for the part. There are no new Madonna compositions on this record, in contrast to other cinematic projects she has been involved with. Her musical contribution is to sing on 15 of the 19 tracks. The other principal vocalists featured are Jimmy Nail, Jonathan Pryce and Antonio Banderas. The credits list guitarist Gary Moore as one of the musicians who contributed to the recording. The album carries the note from Madonna "special thanks to Joan Lader for helping me find my voice, to David Caddick for his patience and guidance and to Caresse Henry-Norman for her strength."

Unlike the styles of music Madonna has worked in, this kind of popular musical uses the classical technique of development. With development, a composer takes a theme – a melody or a distinctive phrase – and presents it in a variety of settings, keys and tempos. The central musical theme of Evita is the melody best known as the standard 'Don't Cry For Me Argentina'. This theme can be heard on several tracks. The material embraces a small range of styles, most of which end up being pastiche. Latin American influences mix with orchestral writing, and rock drums and guitar parts. The album tells the rags-to-riches story of Eva Peron, wife of the Argentine dictator Peron, her huge popularity, her fall from grace and her transformation into a legend. Shorn of any real political dimension, the story is vulgar and pretentious: a charismatic woman becomes a monster of vanity and pride, for whom it is difficult to feel any sympathy.

Madonna felt very strongly that this role was for her and that she would shine in it. There are a number of moments when the lyrics throw up phrases which obviously have resonance for Madonna's life. It isn't hard to see why she was drawn to the role. However, the combination of two such giant female egos is sometimes overpowering. On a musical level, the material is quite different to Madonna's own records and at times is the most challenging music she has sung since the Stephen Sondheim songs of *Dick Tracy*. The irony of this record is that she turns in a competent performance with material that is often inferior to the best of her own songs. Only two are songs effective enough to stand on their own – 'Another Suitcase In Another Hall' and the theatrical 'Don't Cry For Me Argentina'. The rest are largely concerned with the unfolding narrative of Eva's rise to fame and therefore do not stand alone as separate pieces.

Although her role in the film brought her the kind of critical notices for which she had always dreamed, *Evita* does nothing whatsoever for her own musical development.

Only the tracks on which Madonna is audibly present are listed. All tracks are composed by Andrew Lloyd Weber and Tim Rice. There is a two-CD version of this, called *Evita: The Motion Picture Soundtrack* (Warner 9362-46346-2). It includes the following additional tracks: Circus in Buenos Aires / The Lady's Got Potential / Charity Concert / The Art of the Possible / Hello and Goodbye / On the Balcony of the Casa Rosada parts 1 and 2 / Rainbow Tour / The Actress Hasn't Learned the Lines (You'd Like To Hear) / Partido Feminista / Your Little Body's Breaking Down / Latin Chant.

OH WHAT A CIRCUS

MADONNA only sings a few lines in this number. This track is a sort of grand introduction to the whole, working the main 'Don't Cry For Me' tune in various ways. There are several Spanish guitars helping the atmosphere along, as Banderas takes the lead vocal. This is mostly an up tempo version of the melody of 'Don't Cry For Me Argentina'. The lyric looks back on Eva Peron's life after her funeral, taking the view that her life has been a circus. There is a choir passage in the middle. The lyric then says that Eva has let down her people. There's a sudden change of rhythm and tempo for a rock passage with a few tumbling piano glissandos. "She didn't say much but she said it loud" is a phrase that some think might well apply to Madonna or this musical. The choir

returns almost unaccompanied toward the end, again on the main melody. This then leads to a slow orchestral passage again using the main theme, with plenty of gongs and timpani. Madonna takes up the main tune at this point, "share my glory / so share my coffin". It's the spurious democratic notion of "we're all stars".

EVA AND MAGALDI/EVA BEWARE OF THE CITY

A SOUL shuffle starts this off with funky bass and distorted electric guitar. In parts, this is a tricky melody. It narrates Eva's move away from home, from her poor beginnings, which is a clear echo of Madonna's own humble beginnings. The number breaks down into different sections, with or without percussion. The second half –

'Eva Beware of the City' – is a warning from the men about life, a warning about what happens to strangers who go to the big city. Eva is also warned because she is a woman, which is another factor to excite Madonna's identification. "Screw the middle class" says Madonna at one point, in a solo vocal passage. Then the tempo picks up again.

Madonna sounds a bit strait-jacketed by the requirements of the track. The many changes make it a demanding number.

BUENOS AIRES

EVA ARRIVES in the big city, looking for excess. A train horn sounds through a flicker of light guitars and Latin percussion and drumming. The verse is twice interrupted by sudden stops. The passage where the melody takes Madonna into a higher range makes her sound more like the artist of her solo records. There's a sinister theme on heavy guitar and trumpets with some discordant playing that comes across a bit like a collision between John Barry and a Latin salsa band. "Put me down for a lifetime of success" sings Madonna, bringing in a touch of star quality. We get the message.

ANOTHER SUITCASE IN ANOTHER HALL

THIS SONG was a hit single for Barbara Dickson in 1977 and is the other famous song from the musical. Madonna sings this in a gentler voice than she would usually employ in her material.

Again, Eva is the centre of attention but the lyric does allow a transfer of meaning outside of the context of her story. Part of the song's popularity lies in the way it finds an image – the suitcase in the hall – to express the nomadic nature of modern civilisation, the feeling of urban rootlessness that many people experience. The theme of constant moving strikes a resonant note. The song is generally carried by strings and some subdued acoustic guitars. This gave Madonna another hit single in 1997.

GOODNIGHT AND THANK YOU

THIS STARTS with a real brassy swagger like circus music. Flutes trill, horns and strings carry the main tune. Eva is now being photographed and is in all the magazines. This is the end of a love affair and a very bright and breezy end too. Madonna sings some passages solo and shares others with Antonio Banderas. There's one bizarre sequence singing the praise of soap, where Madonna shares the tune with several female backing voices.

I'D BE SURPRISINGLY GOOD FOR YOU

THE DRAMATIC moment when Eva meets her husband and her political destiny is assured. Initially they seem to inhabit separate lives: he is a soldier and she is an actress.

This begins as a kind of recitative and then leads into a gentle ballad with flute and classical guitar, and subdued strings. Congas take this into a sexy shuffle. Madonna turns in a more expressive vocal to communicate the tender excitement of the first encounter. Eva doesn't want a sudden brief fling. There's a sax solo over some fretless bass to sustain the smoochy mood. Banderas alternates verses with some lines about his own character's feelings. It ends quite abruptly leading on with the story, reminding us this is a musical, not a pop album.

PERON'S LATEST FLAME

PERON'S military character and position are signalled by the martial drum beat and a brass section pounding away. Banderas takes up the initial lyric, registering the fact that certain classes have taken against Eva. Her lover registers this but disapproves. This has a strong rhythm, with the lyric reinforced by some massed singing from the backing chorus of male voices voicing the massed disapproval of Eva. Listening on headphones you'll hear some stereo tom-tom rolls and a few seconds of tired Seventies prog-rock with a Rick Wakeman-esque synth solo. There are some witty lines from lyricist Tim Rice. The people get to call Eva a bitch and a slut. Eva complains about being only an actress, and wants more influence.

A NEW ARGENTINA

ELECTRIC guitars and three-time start this Queen-esque bit of stadium rock with massed singing. Eva supports her lover's political ambition. This is supposed to be a popular uprising hymn but it comes across as pretty jaded exercise. Madonna sings this quite aggressively with a growl in her voice. The middle of the track quietens down, moves away from the rock mode for a while and then crashes back into the chromatic riff and loud drums when Peron resigns from the army and marches in front of the workers. It builds to a big vocal climax with Madonna's voice singing over the ranks of the others.

DON'T CRY FOR ME ARGENTINA

THE MOST famous track on the album, a hit for Julie Covington in 1977 (who took it to number 1 in the UK charts) and for The Shadows who recorded an instrumental version of it in 1979. The song starts with strings only, to which a harp is soon added. The lyrics again have many resonant phrases, as Madonna uses the song to make some sort of oblique statement about herself. She sings it competently, just occasionally slipping into a shriller sound, employing vibrato throughout. The second verse brings in light percussion with acoustic guitar. The second chorus swells and becomes louder and more rhythmic. Some of the lines in the second verse are very ironic, for example, the one about being an illusion. Cymbal crashes usher in the last statement of the theme and then it fades away. How does one account for the popularity of this song? A politician comes clean in some vague gesture of humility?

An unholy mix of undissolved fake humility, popularism and egoism casseroled in a suitably grandiose setting, in which the egoism of Madonna collides with the egoism of Eva Peron and creates something of a black hole for anyone else in the vicinity.

HIGH FLYING, ADORED

THANKFULLY we go onto a smaller scale for this pleasant enough pop song. Banderas sings the first verse of this, a fantasy of the bedroom and a saint, a backstreet girl etc. Moments of this song are Elton John like in style. When Madonna sings the line "you did it all at 26" we have another parallel with her own life. Here Eva is at the top of her cycle of fame, but the male vocal warns Eva of what is to come, how the people will turn against her. Madonna enters on a change of a key, the local girl makes good. The song has the nauseating narcissistic air of self-applause which permeates the entire musical.

RAINBOW HIGH

THIS IS A slightly quicker track with a minor chord sequence. Fame and success intoxicate Eva, who is now in full Marie-Antoinette-Let-Them-Eat-Cake mode. She wants to reinvent herself as a star, a goddess. The people want entertainment and she wants it too. They need their escape from a life of grinding poverty and political betrayal, and Eva needs her French gowns and a make-over! They need their escape and so do I. Drums, horns, strings and electric guitar are the main featured instruments, carrying some contrived lyrics and some contrived leaps in the melody. If you can tear yourself from the copy of Marx and Engels that you've probably grabbed already, you'll notice a change of key and a salsa section at the end. One small step for the Argentine people, one huge leap for Eva's wardrobe and shoe rack.

WALTZ FOR EVA AND CHE

AS THE title promises, this is indeed a waltz. Even dictators must dance occasionally. He sings the first verse, accusing Eva of betraying the people. She sings the second verse in justification. It's a view of politics as a branch of popular entertainment. It is not made clear who the Che of the title is. As he is leaving she mocks him. This being a musical, they do it all in perfect harmonies. The music is quite incidental to the lyric. It climaxes with a pompous main theme complete with oompah brass, timpani and quite a few clichés. It breaks down into a string passage where Eva laments the fact that she's growing old. The guitar briefly plays a tune which is very similar to The Shadows' 'Theme For Young Lovers' only not so good.

YOU MUST LOVE ME

MADONNA starts this with a solo vocal and then sings a ballad over a piano. In the chorus a cello lends mournful support. The lyric wonders how they keep the dream alive. How indeed? And do we care? The impatient listener familiar with Madonna's output will be provoked to compare this with something like 'Promise To Try' which is much, much better. The song makes no specific reference to Eva so the song is detachable from the musical. It is, at least, short. This was a hit single for Madonna in 1996.

EVA'S FINAL BROADCAST

MADONNA starts this off in a similar vein, with sombre horns and woodwind. The melody has some strange twists in it. Eva is ill and dying. The choirs enter singing "Evita" repeatedly. This fades away and Madonna continues with the main 'Don't Cry For Me' tune. There is a reprise of this song with different lyrics as 'Eva'.

There's an impressive bit of tearful vocal from Madonna on this – lack of control or consummate control? The massed voices return with a funereal passage in Spanish with rolling drums and strummed acoustic guitars in the background. Musically speaking, this is one of the more interesting passages. The choir fades away to bring in a piano rumble and a male voice singing the 'Argentina' tune.

LAMENT

MADONNA sings over a classical guitar, as Eva looks back on her life and fame with a degree of self-absorption which puts the forces of gravity to flight. Madonna comes up with a very quavering vocal, consequently loosing some of the notes. Some of these lines are half-spoken. Then with a very vulgar orchestral crash there is the grand instrumental finale, timpani thunder, brass rumbles etc. Then a quieter passage in which classical guitar and harp bring in Banderas to sing over Eva's grave. There is plenty of sentimental stuff about how soon the light has gone, and a reprise of 'Rainbow High', given a mocking quality. It fades out with a strange sense of anti-climax, certainly a not very effective end to the album, and leaves you full of profound thoughts like... where are my car keys?

COMPILATIONS

The Immaculate Collection

Sire WX 370, CD 7599 26440-2; The Royal Box 7599 26493-2

Released November 1990

'Holiday', 'Lucky Star', 'Borderline', 'Like A Virgin', 'Material Girl', 'Crazy For You', 'Into The Groove', 'Live To Tell', 'Papa Don't Preach', 'Open Your Heart', 'La Isla Bonita, 'Like A Prayer', 'Express Yourself', 'Cherish/Vogue', 'Justify My Love', 'Rescue Me'

THREE YEARS WERE TO ELAPSE BETWEEN 'LIKE A PRAYER' AND ITS FOLLOW-UP studio album, (not counting the music inspired by *Dick Tracy* which clearly represents something of a side alley away from Madonna's main line of development). With the end of the Eighties, the material girl decided to take stock. The result was this massively successful greatest hits compilation, wittily entitled *The Immaculate Collection*, a title guaranteed to have church-goers fuming. This was Madonna's Greatest Hits Volume 1. Unlike most greatest hits, this collection really lived up to the description. All the previously available tracks were high-charting singles. In fact, Madonna had had so many hits that there wasn't room for all of them. Thus, 'Causing A Commotion', 'Angel', 'Dear Jessie', 'Dress You Up', 'Hanky Panky', 'Look Of Love', 'Gambler' and 'Who's That Girl' are left out in the rain. On the marketing front, this also appeared as 'The Royal Box', a box set in satin digipak with a video, poster and postcards.

As it stands, the double album gives a vivid sense of the rapid development of the sound of her records, from the brassy disco of the first three to the orchestrated drama of 'Like A Prayer' and the sunny bounce and richness of 'Cherish'. Mysteriously, the album carries a dedication to the Pope. Sales were greatly boosted by the furore over the video to 'Justify My Love', which was promptly banned by MTV and, as a result, became a must-have item. The album came out 13 November. By December 6 the video was in the shops selling for just under $10. By February 1991 it became the first video short to sell 400,000 copies. The double album did extremely well, reaching the number 1 position in charts all over the world and exceeding seven times platinum sales. The tracks were re-mixed in 'Q'-sound, a process supposed to give the illusion of quadraphonic sound from a stereo mix. Apparently Madonna needed some coaxing to release this.

Of course, plenty of people already owned these tracks, so to entice them to invest in this collection whoever put it together adopted the old trick of spicing it up with two new songs.

JUSTIFY MY LOVE
(Lenny Kravitz/with additional lyrics by Madonna)

HAVING previously collaborated with Prince, Madonna here finds herself in bed – er... musically speaking – with the Dreadlocked Princeling and Guardian Of Analogue Recording, Lenny Kravitz, who had risen to fame toward the end of the Eighties with several hit singles and two albums' worth of Sixties-inspired rock-funk. Surprisingly, 'Justify My Love' comes across as an up-to-date hip-hop dance track. The elements are simple enough: a drum loop that repeats for the duration of the song, a bass part, and a descending four chord sequence moving from F♯ minor to B minor.

There's a haunting bare perfect fifth held on keyboard and subjected to phasing that could have escaped from a Roxy Music record. There's a judicious amount of vocals a la Jane Birkin in heavy breathing mode, as Madonna mostly talks her way through the song in her best dominatrix voice. Fortunately, this rap is decorated with a wordless vocal melody which has a bewitching quality when juxtaposed with the spoken hook on the chorus. The track doesn't exactly go anywhere, but it creates a hypnotic atmo-sphere which supports the imagery of the lyric.

'Justify My Love' points her musical direction into the Nineties, and as such is a pivotal record, giving her old disco sound the kiss of death. 'Express Yourself' made up the B-side.

'Justify My Love' had a suitably sexy black and white video of couples of contrasting sexual persuasions in a hotel, which gave Madonna a chance to show off the black items in her lingerie drawer. An MTV official allegedly said, 'I can't believe she thought we'd ever show this.' Madonna appeared on a TV show called *Nightline* to explain the video, stating that it was meant to be educational. One further aspect of 'Justify My Love' caused controversy. Kravitz's friend Ingrid Chavez, a singer-songwriter, claimed that he had appropriated what was really her song, and that only the title phrase was his, and that Madonna's part in the song was merely to change one line. An out-of-court settlement resulted in Chavez receiving a portion of the royalties. The rhythm track was supposed to have been borrowed from Public Enemy's 'Security Of The First World' and brought a response record by the Young Black Teenagers called 'To My Donna'. The Beast Mix of the song had Madonna reciting

Revelations 2:9, which drew charges of anti-Semitism. Phew! Has Madonna ever thought of doing something safer... like bee-keeping, wasp clearance, or snake-charming?

RESCUE ME
(Madonna/Shep Pettibone)

NOTHING to do with Fontella Bass's Sixties hit, this is a faster dance-track with a spoken intro and many chest-beating declarations of the power of luurve. The overall sound is reminiscent of Yazoo and other Eighties disco acts. Madonna starts to growl some of the lines toward the end, which was ill-advised. The arrangement is thick, with loads of backing vocals. The clichéd lyric makes heavy weather of the drowning metaphor, along with allusions to sending out an SOS on loan from Edwin Starr's Motown hit, and another to Aretha's 'Respect'. The best thing about this track is the ending: the instruments fade away to leave the backing vocals on their own and then the sound of thunder and rain. Released as a single with 'Spotlight' on the B-side, 'Rescue Me' was subjected to no less than eight re-mixes!

Something To Remember

Maverick 9362 46100-1; CD 9362-46100-2; Released November 1995

'I Want You'. 'I'll Remember', 'Take A Bow', 'You'll See Me', 'Crazy For You', 'This Used To Be My Playground', 'Live To Tell', 'Love Don't Live Here Anymore', 'Something To Remember', 'Forbidden Love', 'One More Chance', 'Rain', 'Oh Father', 'I Want You'

A KIND OF SUCCESSOR TO *THE IMMACULATE COLLECTION*, THIS THIRD COLLECTION of Madonna's career was an attempt to draw attention to her music (as opposed to everything else which drew attention to Madonna), especially her less dance-oriented material. The sleeve-note had her explaining: "So much controversy has swirled around my career this past decade that very little attention ever gets paid to my music. The songs are all but forgotten. While I have no regrets regarding the choices I've made artistically, I've learned to appreciate the idea of doing things in a simpler way. So without a lot of fanfare, without any distractions, I present to you this collection of ballads. Some are old, some are new. All of them are from my heart."

Although Madonna is right in suggesting that little attention gets paid to her music, it must be said that the blame for this can be laid entirely at her feet. Controversy swirled about her career largely because she stirred it. To adapt an old blues metaphor, if you want people to appreciate your living room, don't spend all your time in the kitchen.

So, how successful is *Something To Remember*, both in these terms – refocussing on Madonna's music – and as an album in its own right? There is no doubt that the song selection creates a unity of mood. The music remains downbeat, atmospheric, emotionally introverted throughout. You can play this late at night or on Sunday morning and it won't spoil the mellow vibes. The earliest track chosen from Madonna's career is 'Love Don't Live Here Anymore', remixed by David Reitzas. It still sounds weak because of the relatively inexperienced vocal by Madonna, which shows that her voice doesn't take to being pushed to get more aggression. Several previously uncollected singles are gathered onto album for the first time, along with three new songs. The emphasis here is very much on Madonna as a singer, rather than controversialist, so the album lacks the overtly sexual themes of the previous two studio albums. Designed as the Madonna album which would appeal to a wide audience, the packaging featured red roses on the inside, a yellow-gold flower on the back, and Madonna in a white dress leaning against a wall in a pose of romantic loss or absorption, or maybe with a headache.

I WANT YOU
(WITH MASSIVE ATTACK)
(Leon Ware/T-Boy Ross)

A LONG introduction starts this song, with a hip-hop drum with exceptional emphasis on the bass, and a semi-tone string figure. Madonna sings this song of desire in a slow, languid manner, her vocal right to the front of the mix. He doesn't want her anymore but she is determined to change his mind. This could almost be the theme to a James Bond film. The second chorus comes in with a swirl of harp. The drum loop goes on repeating, complete with a strange bleeping noise on top of it, which has roughly the same effect as a telephone ringing when you're otherwise engaged late at night.

There's not much melody for Madonna to get her teeth into. Her singing is supported by some quietly spoken passages, which come in again during the sparse bridge. Unrequited love is a fantasy, says the lyric. It remains a long, somewhat hollow and chill confection hugely overlong at six minutes. The musical pretensions of the melody and chord sequence are at odds with the drum loop which just goes on repeating throughout.

I'LL REMEMBER
*(Pat Leonard/Madonna/
Richard Page)*

THE THEME song from the film With Honors, and amazingly, one of Madonna's biggest ever singles. This is altogether a stronger cut, written in the style of a late Seventies AOR track by Boston or Foreigner but without the guitars, arranged by a bunch of dance/soul buffs and slowed down. In place of heavy guitars, a steadily reverberating synth keyboard pulses throughout the track like a heartbeat. The beginning is striking because of the C major – D major chord change at the start. D major is the actual key, C is the chord on the flattened seventh and is unusual used in this way. Backing vocals on the later choruses add some nice support along with a few strings cascading down just before the third chorus. Lyrically, Madonna looks back on a good love affair. In parts this could almost be by Prince. The choruses use a very popular chord sequence to good effect, not just repeating it as a turnaround. For the second verse the drums come in much stronger. This is a very typical late Seventies song apart from the arrangement and the very heavy low bass. Here Madonna's voice is less to the forefront and almost overshadowed by the keyboards. There's no climax or sudden dramatics - the track just fades out without histrionics.

YOU'LL SEE
(Madonna/David Foster)

A REITERATED low bass, wind-chimes and the occasional twist of Spanish guitar introduce this sombre moody E minor ballad, whose lyric tells a story of defiant perseverance. The singer makes a quiet but firm declaration that she will survive the break-up of a love affair and much to her former partner's surprise will go on to greater things. The chord changes of the progression and the turns in the melody give Madonna a chance to put her voice to work. There's a much greater rate of harmonic change than on the other tracks which adds to the interest. At the minute mark the percussion comes in to move the song along with a controlled sense of drama. The phrase "somehow, somewhere" makes 'You'll See' momentarily sound like a song from a musical. There are some attractive bits of additional tremolo guitar sounding like broken glass. The string synth has a nice tense two-note motif. The drums come in after the first chorus which adds more power to the track. The arrangement is slowly building all the time. The second chorus has Madonna harmonising with herself and the track concludes in a pleasingly undramatic way, winding down through the last few bars which bring in a few more harmonic changes.

This was the lead single from the compilation, followed by 'Oh

Father' which had only reached number 20 in the US in 1989. Asked if it was a song about revenge, Madonna replied, "No, it's about empowering yourself."

THIS USED TO BE MY PLAYGROUND
(Madonna/Shep Pettibone)

THIS IS gorgeous. This song was featured over the closing credits of the film *A League Of Their Own* in which Madonna appeared as a member of a struggling team in the All-American Girls Professional Baseball League in the Forties. The film itself was entertaining and Madonna's part as the spirited but risqué May was one of her more successful film roles. The song appropriately reinforces the strongly nostalgic feel of the film's closing scenes where the women, now much older, are reunited in a newly opened museum display dedicated to the women's league. The song turned up again on the *Barcelona Gold* Olympics compilation. It gave her a US number 1 and reached the top three in the UK.

A previously uncollected single, this has a pretty keyboard intro before a swell of strings usher in a slow song in which Madonna revisits her place of childhood dreams. The chord sequence has a pleasing sense of the unexpected in terms of where it starts and pauses, moving from Eb down to Gm and momentarily to F major only to back off again. The whole is supported by some good string writing. This is very much in the mould of 'Like A Prayer's exploration of childhood. She is torn between the pull of the past and letting go and concludes that letting go is too much to ask.

A very lush romantic track with some nice twists in the melody, which seems to keep peaking, subsiding, and peaking again. The structure of the song has a seamless quality, where the chorus and verse flow into one another. There's a subdued but expressive vocal from Madonna, a string-led orchestral break, and some nice backing vocals on the third verse. The track comes to a sudden ending on a suspended orchestral chord and backing vocals, expressing the desire (probably addressed to her mother) "wishing you were here with me". Listen carefully to the last double-tracked phrase and you'll hear her voice produce just a touch of roughness through emotion. The best track on the album, and one of Madonna's very best recordings and most expressive singles.

ONE MORE CHANCE
(Madonna/David Foster)

THIS TRACK hinges on the foregrounding of a finger-picked acoustic guitar in the style that made Extreme's 'More Than Words' a hit. The verse is in F major, the chorus leans toward D minor, the middle 8 goes to D major which is a surprise and it ends in D major too. It's something of a shock to hear

Madonna's voice in the middle of such an 'organic' arrangement, rather than surrounded, as it usually is, by the normal synths and sequencing, supported by guitar and some subdued strings. There are plenty of chord changes as Madonna puts herself in the role of chanteuse trying to win her lost lover back, though unfortunately the lyrics (like the title) are rather bland. Her singing is perhaps lacking in the confidence and improvisation needed to make this kind of material really come alive. It's an example Madonna not taking chances, where taking chances might lift the performance without swamping it. The last phrase of the chorus has a delicious interval leap up on "if you care for me". There's a nice harmony generated between the guitar and her voice and a brief excursion into a different key for the middle eight. With a brief pause for her solo voice, and a couple more guitar chords it's gone, resolving the minor tension of the song onto a major chord.

I WANT YOU (ORCHESTRAL MIX)

IT'S THAT dreaded word 'mix' again. For this version (which closes the album), the original drum-track, percussion and bass are removed. This version starts with low sustained strings and Madonna's wordless singing. She starts the first verse with only a low string bass line counter-pointing her voice. Gradually the rest of the string parts are brought into the mix. In some ways the removal of the looped drum track liberates the music from that fatal element of mechanised repetition which dogs the opening cut. You hear some harp and brass touches in the backing which are not so obvious on track 1. There's a dramatic moment toward the end where the strings cease and leave her voice unaccompanied and then they come back in for the slow gentle fade. This version loses about twenty seconds to the earlier version and I would say is the marginally better of the two

GHV2

Maverick / Warner Bros 9362-48000-2 November 2001

'Deeper And Deeper', 'Erotica', 'Human Nature', 'Secret', 'Don't Cry For Me Argentina', 'Bedtime Story', 'The Power Of Good-Bye', 'Beautiful Stranger', 'Frozen', 'Take A Bow', 'Ray Of Light', 'Don't Tell Me', 'What It Feels Like For A Girl', 'Drowned World', 'Substitute For Love', 'Music'

THIS IS THE FOLLOW-UP TO THE ENORMOUSLY SUCCESSFUL *IMMACULATE Collection*, drawing its tracks from the *Erotica* album onwards to create a

Madonna Greatest Hits from the Nineties. Like its predecessor it does not present every chart hit she had.

There is one previously uncollected track:

BEAUTIFUL STRANGER
(Madonna/William Orbit)

THIS TRACK was a one-off composed for the Austin Powers film *The Spy Who Shagged Me* (1999) and won a Grammy for its writers. The intent was to evoke Sixties pop/psychedelia which it does reasonably well. It opens with a clever intro that alludes to The Doors' 'Light My Fire' and The Beatles' 'Lucy In The Sky With Diamonds'. At 1:06 there's a hint of mellotron recorders/flutes, such as were featured on Sixties classics like 'Strawberry Fields Forever' and 'Fool On The Hill'. This is strong enough to be worthy of inclusion on *Ray Of Light* when it gets remastered.

MISCELLANEOUS

SO FAR THE MAIN COMPILATIONS OF MADONNA'S WORK ARE *THE IMMACULATE Conception*, *Something To Remember* and *GHV2*. Madonna's song 'Ain't No Big Deal' which was the b-side of her single 'Papa Don't Preach' was included on the album *Revenge Of The Killer B's* (Warner Bros 1984). The soundtrack to the film *Vision Quest* included two songs, 'Crazy For You' and 'Gambler'. The album *A Very Special Christmas* (A&M, 1987) included the track 'Santa Baby'. The song 'Goodbye To Innocence' can be found on *Just Say Roe* (Sire, 1994). Madonna provided guest vocals (as 'mystery girl') on the song 'In The Closet' from Michael Jackson's *Dangerous* (Epic 1991). Her version of 'I Want You' features on *Inner City Blues: The Music of Marvin Gaye* (1995) and a song called 'Freedom' is on the 1997 *Carnival (Rainforest Foundation Concert)* 1997) album. She sang a duet 'Be Careful (Cuidado Con Mi Corazon)' with Ricky Martin on his eponymous album. The soundtrack album to the film *The Next Best Thing* (2000) includes 'American Pie' and one otherwise unavailable song, 'Time Stood Still'.

One hoary chestnut which needs to be avoided is *anything* attributed to Madonna and Otto Von Wernherr, for example *In The Beginning* (Receiver Records, 1987, CDKNOB 1) which has appeared under a number of titles like *The Early Years*. Before Madonna had made any records of her own she sang backing vocals on these tracks by Von Wernherr: 'Wild Dancing', 'Cosmic Climb' and 'We Are The Gods'. This was in 1981. Some of this material has appeared as 12" singles. It appeared as *Best Of And The Rest Of* (Trojan Records, 1989, CD AR1005) and *The Early Years: Madonna: Give It To Me*

(Receiver 1991, RR CD 144). Tracks on this are 'Give It To Me', 'Shake', 'Get Down', 'Time To Dance', 'Wild Dancing', 'Let's Go Dancing', 'We Are The Gods', 'Cosmic Climb', 'On The Street' and 'Oh My'. The packaging is a blatant cash-in on Madonna's success, designed to make the purchaser think they are buying material which will feature Madonna upfront as the main singer, taken from some rare archive of unreleased recordings. It really isn't worth your time, unless you like Euro-disco.

The *Early Years* material has recently appeared as a two-disc set on Sanctuary/Trojan in 2002 – same eight tracks, numerous mixes. *In The Beginning* (Gravity, 1998) features other early recordings in a variety of mixes: 'Crimes Of Passion', 'Everybody '97', 'Ain't No Big Deal '97', 'Laugh To Keep From Crying', 'Burning Up', 'Ain't No Big Deal '81', 'Everybody '81', 'Stay '81', and 'Don't You Know?'.

The Complete Madonna (2002) is a three-CD set of interviews, comprising *Maximum Madonna*, *Absolute Madonna* and *More Maximum Madonna*, with two mini-posters and five postcards. There is no music on this set.

Her first three official albums were repackaged as a box-set for a reduced price by WEA in 1999. Other repackaging has been undertaken in different territories but this is usually cosmetic only. In France *You Can Dance* was boxed up with *Erotica*. In 2001 her Eighties albums appeared in remastered form with the addition of a couple of different mixes of some of the tracks. The tracks 'Holiday', 'True Blue', 'Who's That Girl' and 'Causing A Commotion' were released as a four-track CD single called 'The Holiday Collection'.

If you fancy the idea of Madonna's music arranged for classical instruments try *Material Girl: the Royal Philharmonic Orchestra Plays the Music of Madonna* (Music Club, 1998) or *The String Quartet tribute to Madonna* (Vitamin Records, 2002). Various artists try their hand at covering 28 of Madonna's songs on the two volumes of *Virgin Voices: A tribute to Madonna* (Cleopatra, 1999 and 2000).

The Japanese version of *Ray Of Light* has an extra track, 'Has To Be', and the Japanese version of *Music* features an extra song 'Cyber-raga' which was also the B-side to the single 'Music'. Madonna's B-sides are generally either instrumental mixes of the A-side, re-mixes, or album tracks. Some formats of 'Rain' had a track called 'Up Down Suite' on the B-side. One Madonna single with a B-side unavailable anywhere else is 'Cherish', which is backed by:

SUPERNATURAL THING
(Madonna/Pat Leonard)

FOR A B-side, this is actually not bad at all. Lyrically, it's a tongue-in-cheek story of a ghost lover set to a typical 'Into The Groove' type Madonna rhythm track, with the usual bass synth and drum machine. There's a few seconds of distorted electric guitar at the very beginning before the track kicks in. The verse is in D minor but the chorus is in C minor - an unusual key change and one that adds interest, along with some odd melodic touches. The chorus has a multiple vocal hook and here and there Madonna adds some spoken passages. If you listen carefully to the fade you'll hear an effect known as reverse reverb, which makes voices sound spooky. This is worth hearing. A remix of this track is on the Aids benefit album *Red, Hot + Dance* (Sony 1992).

MADONNA ON VIDEO

THIS SECTION DEALS FIRST WITH MADONNA'S MUSIC VIDEOS AND THEN BRIEFLY with her appearance in films as an actress. Video has been particularly important for her career. Her initial success came only a few years after the establishment of MTV, the 24-hour music TV channel, and in its wake many other exclusively music-oriented channels have been set up. The pop video became an effective way of supporting an artist and plugging a song. It was less risky than live performance in a TV studio and, some might say, more interesting than watching the artist mime to a backing track. For an image conscious performer like Madonna, video was extremely important as it enabled her to keep control of how she was seen in the media. It made it possible for her to invite comparisons with Hollywood stars of the past by occasionally borrowing ideas from old films. It also meant she could be seen by millions she could never hope to reach through the spirit-sapping process of touring. These titles do not include all the promotional films made to illustrate her singles; there is plenty of stuff in the can which has been seen on TV and in-store over the years but has not yet been collected for official release.

Two documentaries which are available are *Madonna: the Unauthorised Biography* (DCL 1048, 1993, 60 mins) and *Madonna: The Real Story* (Wienerworld Classic, 1991, 48 mins).

MADONNA
Warner Music Video WMV 3;
February 1985; 18 minutes

TRACKS: 'Burning Up', 'Borderline', 'Lucky Star', 'Like A Virgin'

THIS comprises of her first four promotions, in chronological order. With the exception of 'Borderline', the clips are also available on The Immaculate Collection

THE VIRGIN TOUR - LIVE
Warner Music Video 938 105-3;
December 1985; 50 minutes

TRACKS: 'Dress You Up', 'Holiday', 'Into The Groove', 'Everybody', 'Gambler', 'Lucky Star', 'Crazy For You', 'Over And Over', 'Like A Virgin', 'Material Girl'

THIS footage was taken from a concert in her hometown of Detroit in 1985, during her first world tour.

CIAO ITALIA - LIVE FROM ITALY
Warner Reprise Video - 938 141-3;
June 1988; 100 minutes (Also
available as a laser disc 980 141-3
From October 1989)

TRACKS: 'Open Your Heart', 'Lucky Star', 'True Blue', 'Papa Don't Preach', 'White Heat', 'Causing A Commotion', 'The Look Of Love', 'Dress You Up-Material Girl-Like A Virgin', 'Where's The Party', 'Live To Tell', 'Into The Groove', 'La Isla Bonita', 'Who's That Girl', 'Holiday'

THIS footage came from two concerts in Italy on Madonna's 1987 world tour. It shows Madonna using more costume changes and choreography than ever before. A *Ciao Italia* DVD version was released in 1999.

PAPA DON'T PREACH
Sire / WEA laser disc 925 681-2

TRACKS: Papa Don't Preach', 'Papa Don't Preach' (Audio Only 7" Edit). 'Papa Don't Preach' (Audio Only 12"). 'Pretender' (Audio Only)

THE IMMACULATE COLLECTION
Warner Music Vision 7599 38214-3;
November 1989; 55 Minutes

TRACKS: 'Lucky Star', 'Borderline', 'Like A Virgin', 'Material Girl', 'Papa Don't Preach', 'Open Your Heart', 'La Isla Bonita', 'Like A Prayer', 'Express Yourself', 'Cherish', 'Oh Father', 'Vogue'

THIS was far from being a complete roll-call of the videos of Madonna's numerous hit singles. The audio compilation had been unable to fit all the hits onto a double album and that has more tracks than this. The clip of 'Oh Father' was the rare pick here, originally made to support an American single. If you don't own any Madonna videos, and you'd like to, this is probably the one to start with.

JUSTIFY MY LOVE

Warner Music Vision 7599 38225-3;
January 1991; 13 minutes

TRACKS: 'Justify My Love', 'Vogue'

IT'S HARD to see now why so many worked themselves up into such a lather over the black and white hotel sequence in which Madonna is seen entertaining several friends of various sexual dispositions, all of whom endeavour to tie themselves up in tight corsets; and where she makes love while being watched. It's a video in part about voyeurism, which perhaps conceals the fact that the watcher is implicated in all this voyeurism. The performance of 'Vogue' has Madonna miming in eighteenth-century costume on the 1990 MTV awards.

IN BED WITH MADONNA

The Video Collection MAD 18;
September 1991

TRACKS: 'Papa Don't Preach', 'Express Yourself', 'Oh Father', 'Like A Virgin', 'Promise To Try', 'Like A Prayer', 'Holiday', 'Live To Tell', 'Vogue', 'Causing A Commotion', 'Family Affair-Keep It Together'

ALSO known by the title *Truth Or Dare*, this is the famous account of Madonna's 1990 world tour, complete with lots of backstage and hotel footage, sometimes bringing in the famous, like Warren Beatty, who in one memorable scene com-plains about Madonna's constant desire to be in front of the camera. The most interesting stuff of course ended up on the cutting room floor. The live footage is pretty hot, shot during some of the American Blond Ambition concerts. The version of 'Live A Virgin' is delightfully sleazy. Beware that there is also a certifi-cate 15 version with the more 'adult' scenes taken out.

Madonna commented, "It's worth five years of psychoanalysis. There are some painful moments. I can see all of my extreme behaviour, but I can also see my goodness. Certain people, like my agents, have seen it and said, 'I can't believe you're doing this. If I were you, I'd buy it back and put it in a closet.'"

She told *The Advocate*, "Originally we were going to do a concert film because I was really proud of what I'd done on the stage, and I thought, 'I wish I could capture this on film'. But as I started working with the people, what really inter-ested me were the relationships that were developing between me and the dancers and everybody around. We watched the footage of all the backstage stuff... and I said, 'I couldn't give a shit about the live show. This is life! This is what I want to document.'"

For an insight into life on the road during a major concert series, an insight into Madonna, and for the spectacle of various sizeable egos colliding, this is a must-see. It's not as honest as it purports to be, but it's as close as any performer is likely to let his or her audience.

BLOND AMBITION WORLD TOUR LIVE
Pioneer Video laser disc PMLB 00041; November 1991;

TRACKS: 'Express Yourself', 'Open Your Heart', 'Causing A Commotion', 'Where's The Party', 'Like A Virgin', 'Live To Tell-Oh Father', 'Papa Don't Preach', 'Sooner Or Later', 'Hanky Panky', 'Now I'm Following You', 'Material Girl', 'Cherish', 'Into The Groove', 'Vogue', 'Holiday', 'Family Affair-Keep It Together'

THIS is a complete concert from Nice recorded on the *Blond Ambition* tour.

MADONNA: THE VIDEO COLLECTION 1993-99
WEA/Warner Bros VHS / DVD

TRACKS: Bad Girl', 'Fever', 'Rain', 'Secret', 'Take A Bow', 'Bedtime Story', 'Human Nature', 'Love Don't Live Here anymore', 'Frozen', 'Ray Of Light', 'Drowned World', 'Substitute For Love', 'The Power Of Good-Bye', 'Nothing Really Matters', 'Beautiful Stranger'

MADONNA: THE IMMACULATE COLLECTION
WEA/Warner Music Vision 1999 DVD 7599-38195-2

DVD includes extra live version of 'Vogue' taken from the 1990 MTV Awards

DROWNED WORLD TOUR
Maverick/Warner Bros 2001 VHS and DVD 7599385582

TRACKS: Drowned World', 'Substitute for Love', ' Impressive Instant ', ' Candy Perfume Girl', 'Beautiful Stranger', 'Ray of Light', 'Paradise (But Not for Me)', 'Frozen', 'Open Your Heart Swell', 'Nobody's Perfect', 'Mer Girl (Part 1)', 'Sky Fits Heaven', 'Mer Girl (Part 2)', ' I Deserve It', 'Don't Tell Me', 'Human Nature', 'The Funny Song', 'Secret', 'Gone', 'Don't Cry for Me Argentina (instrumental)', 'Lo Que Siente la Mujer (What It Feels Like For A Girl)', 'La Isla Bonita', 'Holiday', 'Music'

'Music' (2001) and 'What It Feels Like For A Girl' (2001) were both released as DVD singles.

FILM APPEARANCES
MADONNA can be seen acting (and occasionally singing) in the following films:

A Certain Sacrifice (1980), *Crazy For You/Vision Quest* (1985), *Desperately Seeking Susan* (1986), *Shanghai Surprise* (1986), *Who's That Girl* (1987), *Bloodhounds of Broadway* (1988), *Dick Tracy* (1991), *A League Of Their Own* (1992), *Body Of Evidence* (1993), *Dangerous Game* (1993), *Four Rooms* (1995), *Blue In The Face* (1995), *and Evita* (1997).

Index